About This Series

The "Classic Retold" series started as a way of telling classics for the modern reader—being careful to preserve the themes and integrity of the original. Whether you want to understand Shakespeare a little more or are trying to get a better grasps of the Greek classics, there is a book waiting for you!

The series is expanding every month. Visit BookCaps.com to see all the books in the series, and while you are there join the Facebook page, so you are first to know when a new book comes out.

Characters

KING RICHARD THE SECOND

JOHN OF GAUNT, Duke of Lancaster - uncle to the King

EDMUND LANGLEY, Duke of York - uncle to the King

HENRY, surnamed BOLINGBROKE, Duke of Hereford, son ofJohn of Gaunt, afterwards King Henry IV

DUKE OF AUMERLE, son of the Duke of York

THOMAS MOWBRAY, Duke of Norfolk

DUKE OF SURREY

EARL OF SALISBURY

EARL BERKELEY

BUSHY - Favorites of King Richard

BAGOT - Favorites of King Richard

GREEN -Favorites of King Richard

EARL OF NORTHUMBERLAND

HENRY PERCY, surnamed HOTSPUR, his son

LORD Ross

LORD WILLOUGHBY

LORD FITZWATER

BISHOP OF CARLISLE

ABBOT OF WESTMINSTER

LORD MARSHAL

SIR STEPHEN SCROOP

William Shakespeare's
King Richard the Second
In Plain and Simple English

BOOKCAPS

A SwipeSpeare™ Book
www.SwipeSpeare.com

Table of Contents:

SIR PIERCE OF EXTON

CAPTAIN of a band of Welshmen

TWO GARDENERS

QUEEN to King Richard

DUCHESS OF YORK

DUCHESS OF GLOUCESTER, widow of Thomas of Woodstock,Duke of Gloucester

LADY attending on the Queen

Lords, Heralds, Officers, Soldiers, Keeper, Messenger,Groom, and other Attendants

Act I

SCENE I.

London. The palace

Enter RICHARD, JOHN OF GAUNT, with other NOBLES and attendants

KING RICHARD.
Old John of Gaunt, time-honoured Lancaster,
Hast thou, according to thy oath and band,
Brought hither Henry Hereford, thy bold son,
Here to make good the boist'rous late appeal,
Which then our leisure would not let us hear,
Against the Duke of Norfolk, Thomas Mowbray?

Old John of Gaunt, venerable Lancaster, have you, according to your promise and oath, brought Henry Hereford, your bold son, here to confirm his recent strong accusations, which at the time we hadn't time to listen to, against the Duke of Norfolk, Thomas Mowbray?

GAUNT.
I have, my liege.

I have, my lord.

KING RICHARD.
Tell me, moreover, hast thou sounded him
If he appeal the Duke on ancient malice,
Or worthily, as a good subject should,
On some known ground of treachery in him?

Tell me, furthermore, have you asked him if he's accusing the Duke due to an old grudge, or truly, like a good subject, on genuine grounds of treachery?

GAUNT.
As near as I could sift him on that argument,
On some apparent danger seen in him
Aim'd at your Highness-no inveterate malice.

As far as I could find out on that question, because he felt that there was somehatred in him towards your Highness–there is no grudge.

KING RICHARD.
Then call them to our presence: face to face
And frowning brow to brow, ourselves will hear
The accuser and the accused freely speak.
High-stomach'd are they both and full of ire,
In rage, deaf as the sea, hasty as fire.

Then call them here: I shall hear the accuser and the accused speak freely, face-to-face and frowning brow to brow. They are both high-spirited and full of anger, *when they're raging they are as deaf as the sea, quick as fire.*

Enter BOLINGBROKE and MOWBRAY

BOLINGBROKE.
Many years of happy days befall
My gracious sovereign, my most loving liege!

May my gracious king, my most loving lord, have many years of happy days

MOWBRAY.
Each day still better other's happiness
Until the heavens, envying earth's good hap,
Add an immortal title to your crown!

ahead of him!

*May you increase the happiness of others
every day, until the heavens, jealous of
Earth's good luck, call you to them.*

KING RICHARD.
We thank you both; yet one but flatters us,
As well appeareth by the cause you come;
Namely, to appeal each other of high treason.
Cousin of Hereford, what dost thou object
Against the Duke of Norfolk, Thomas Mowbray?

*I thank you both; but one of you is lying,
you can see that from the reason you are
here; that is, to accuse each other of
high treason. My cousin Hereford, what is
your accusation against the Duke of
Norfolk, Thomas Mowbray?*

BOLINGBROKE.
First-heaven be the record to my speech!
In the devotion of a subject's love,
Tend'ring the precious safety of my prince,
And free from other misbegotten hate,
Come I appellant to this princely presence.
Now, Thomas Mowbray, do I turn to thee,
And mark my greeting well; for what I speak
My body shall make good upon this earth,
Or my divine soul answer it in heaven-
Thou art a traitor and a miscreant,
Too good to be so, and too bad to live,
Since the more fair and crystal is the sky,
The uglier seem the clouds that in it fly.
Once more, the more to aggravate the note,
With a foul traitor's name stuff I thy throat;
And wish-so please my sovereign-ere I move,
What my tongue speaks, my right drawn sword
may prove.

*Firstly, may Heaven witness what I say!
I come into your royal presence as a
witness, caring about the precious safety
of my prince, free of any other illegitimate
grudge. Now, Thomas Mowbray, I turn to
you, and take good note of my greeting;
for what I say I will answer for with my
body upon this earth, or my immortal soul
will answer for it in heaven– you are a
traitor and a villain, too nobly born to be
so, and too bad to live, as the more lovely
and clear the sky is the uglier the clouds
in it seem. Once more, to confirm your
disgrace, I stuff the name of traitor into
your throat, and ask–if my King permits–
that before I leave, that I may back up my
words with my sword.*

MOWBRAY.
Let not my cold words here accuse my zeal.
'Tis not the trial of a woman's war,
The bitter clamour of two eager tongues,
Can arbitrate this cause betwixt us twain;
The blood is hot that must be cool'd for this.
Yet can I not of such tame patience boast
As to be hush'd and nought at an to say.
First, the fair reverence of your Highness curbs me
From giving reins and spurs to my free speech;
Which else would post until it had return'd
These terms of treason doubled down his throat.

*Don't assume the coldness of my words
indicates a lack of passion. The argument
between the two of us can't be decided the
way women do, shouting bitter words at
each other; blood must be spilled to
settle this. But I'm not going to pretend
I'm so calm that I will stand here and
say nothing. Firstly, my respect for your
Highness stops me from giving my speech
rein, because otherwise I would go on
until I had shoved that accusation of*

Setting aside his high blood's royalty,
And let him be no kinsman to my liege,
I do defy him, and I spit at him,
Call him a slanderous coward and a villain;
Which to maintain, I would allow him odds
And meet him, were I tied to run afoot
Even to the frozen ridges of the Alps,
Or any other ground inhabitable
Where ever Englishman durst set his foot.
Meantime let this defend my loyalty-
By all my hopes, most falsely doth he lie

BOLINGBROKE.
Pale trembling coward, there I throw my gage,
Disclaiming here the kindred of the King;
And lay aside my high blood's royalty,
Which fear, not reverence, makes thee to except.
If guilty dread have left thee so much strength
As to take up mine honour's pawn, then stoop.
By that and all the rites of knighthood else
Will I make good against thee, arm to arm,
What I have spoke or thou canst worst devise.

MOWBRAY.
I take it up; and by that sword I swear
Which gently laid my knighthood on my shoulder
I'll answer thee in any fair degree
Or chivalrous design of knightly trial;
And when I mount, alive may I not light
If I be traitor or unjustly fight!

KING RICHARD.
What doth our cousin lay to Mowbray's charge?
It must be great that can inherit us
So much as of a thought of ill in him.

BOLINGBROKE.
Look what I speak, my life shall prove it true-
That Mowbray hath receiv'd eight thousand nobles
In name of lendings for your Highness' soldiers,
The which he hath detain'd for lewd employments
Like a false traitor and injurious villain.

treason back down his throat; if he wasn't so nobly born, and wasn't related to my lord, I would defy him, and spit on him, call him a slanderous coward, and a villain, and to prove it I would give him odds, and fight him even if I was forced to run on foot to the frozen ridges of the Alps, or any other inhospitable place where an Englishman dares to tread. In the meantime, let this prove my loyalty— I swear on my soul that he is lying.

Pale trembling coward, I throw my glove down, and renounce my kinship to the King; I renounce any claim to my royal blood, which you use as an excuse not to attack me out of fear, not respect. If your guilty fear has left you enough strength to take up my challenge, then pick it up. Through that and all other ceremonies of knighthood I will prove to you, man-to-man, that what I have said is true and that you are lying.

I accept it; and I swear by the sword which was used to confer my knighthood that I will answer it in any fair and chivalrous trial; and once I've started, may I not come out alive, if I am a traitor or am making unjust accusations!

What is my cousin charging Mowbray with? It would have to be very bad to convince me to have the slightest suspicion of him.

Listen to what I say, I'll prove it with my life: Mowbray received eight thousand gold coins to pay your Highness' soldiers, and he used this for improper purposes, like a false traitor, and bloody villain;

Besides, I say and will in battle prove-
Or here, or elsewhere to the furthest verge
That ever was survey'd by English eye-
That all the treasons for these eighteen years
Complotted and contrived in this land
Fetch from false Mowbray their first head and spring.
Further I say, and further will maintain
Upon his bad life to make all this good,
That he did plot the Duke of Gloucester's death,
Suggest his soon-believing adversaries,
And consequently, like a traitor coward,
Sluic'd out his innocent soul through streams of blood;
Which blood, like sacrificing Abel's, cries,
Even from the tongueless caverns of the earth,
To me for justice and rough chastisement;
And, by the glorious worth of my descent,
This arm shall do it, or this life be spent.

besides which I say, and will prove in battle, either here, or anywhere else that has ever been seen by an Englishman, that all the treason for the past eighteen years that has been designed and plotted in this country has had lying Mowbray as its inspiration; furthermore I will say, and will prove by taking his bad life as punishment, that he plotted the death of the Duke of Gloucester, inciting his credulous adversaries, and subsequently, like a cowardly traitor, slaughtered that innocent soul with horrible bloodshed, and that blood now cries out from the speechless depths of the Earth, like that of Abel, asking me to hand out justice and punishment; and I swear by my noble ancestors that I shall do it, or forfeit my life.

KING RICHARD.
How high a pitch his resolution soars!
Thomas of Norfolk, what say'st thou to this?

How determined he is on this! Thomas of Norfolk, what do you say to this?

MOWBRAY.
O, let my sovereign turn away his face
And bid his ears a little while be deaf,
Till I have told this slander of his blood
How God and good men hate so foul a liar.

O, let my King turn his face away, and block his ears for a little while, until I have finished my criticism of this one of royal blood, which will show what a foul liar this man is, hated by God and his fellow man.

KING RICHARD.
Mowbray, impartial are our eyes and ears.
Were he my brother, nay, my kingdom's heir,
As he is but my father's brother's son,
Now by my sceptre's awe I make a vow,
Such neighbour nearness to our sacred blood
Should nothing privilege him nor partialize
The unstooping firmness of my upright soul.
He is our subject, Mowbray; so art thou:
Free speech and fearless I to thee allow.

Mowbray, my eyes and ears are impartial. If he were my brother, even if he were the heir to my kingdom, as he certainly is the son of my father's brother, I swear by the power of my scepter that his close relationship to me will not give him any privileges nor bias the unwavering firmness of my soul. He's my subject, Mowbray; so are you: I give you the righ to speak freely and without fear.

MOWBRAY.

Then, Bolingbroke, as low as to thy heart,
Through the false passage of thy throat, thou liest.
Three parts of that receipt I had for Calais
Disburs'd I duly to his Highness' soldiers;
The other part reserv'd I by consent,
For that my sovereign liege was in my debt
Upon remainder of a dear account
Since last I went to France to fetch his queen:
Now swallow down that lie. For Gloucester's death-
I slew him not, but to my own disgrace
Neglected my sworn duty in that case.
For you, my noble Lord of Lancaster,
The honourable father to my foe,
Once did I lay an ambush for your life,
A trespass that doth vex my grieved soul;
But ere I last receiv'd the sacrament
I did confess it, and exactly begg'd
Your Grace's pardon; and I hope I had it.
This is my fault. As for the rest appeal'd,
It issues from the rancour of a villain,
A recreant and most degenerate traitor;
Which in myself I boldly will defend,
And interchangeably hurl down my gage
Upon this overweening traitor's foot
To prove myself a loyal gentleman
Even in the best blood chamber'd in his bosom.
In haste whereof, most heartily I pray
Your Highness to assign our trial day.

KING RICHARD.
Wrath-kindled gentlemen, be rul'd by me;
Let's purge this choler without letting blood-
This we prescribe, though no physician;
Deep malice makes too deep incision.
Forget, forgive; conclude and be agreed:
Our doctors say this is no month to bleed.
Good uncle, let this end where it begun;
We'll calm the Duke of Norfolk, you your son.

GAUNT.
To be a make-peace shall become my age.
Throw down, my son, the Duke of Norfolk's gage.

*Then, Bolingbroke, your lies come through
your throat from deep down in your heart.
I paid out three quarters of the money I
was given for the war at Calais to his
Highness' soldiers; the other part I kept
with permission, because my royal lord
owed it to me as the remainder of the
money I spent when I went to France for
his marriage negotiations: now take that
lie back. As for the death of Gloucester,
I did not kill him, but to my shame
I did neglect my sworn duty in that case.
My noble Lord of Lancaster,
the honourable father of my enemy,
I did once set an ambush to kill you,
a sin that tormented my sorrowful soul;
but before I last took the sacrament
I confessed it, and expressly asked for
your Grace to pardon me, and I hope you
did. That is my crime–as for the other
accusations, they come from the bitterness
of a villain, a blasphemous and
degenerate traitor, which I will strongly
refute, and I reciprocally throw down my
glove on this terrible traitor's foot,
to prove that I am a loyal gentleman
with honest blood running through my
veins. So that I can prove this I beg that
your Highness will set a day for us to
fight.*

*Angry gentleman, take my advice;
Let's get rid of this fever without letting
blood– this is my prescription, though I'm
not a doctor; great hatred cuts too deeply.
Forgive and forget; stop and be
reconciled: the doctors say this is not a
month for bloodletting. Good uncle, let's
nip this in the bud; I'll calm down the
Duke of Norfolk, you calm down your son.*

*It suits my age to be a peacemaker.
Throw down the Duke of Norfolk's glove,
my son.*

KING RICHARD.
And, Norfolk, throw down his.

And, Norfolk, throw down his.

GAUNT.
When, Harry, when?
Obedience bids I should not bid again.

Come on, Harry, why are you waiting? You should obey, I shouldn't have to ask again.

KING RICHARD.
Norfolk, throw down; we bid.
There is no boot.

Norfolk, throw it down; I order you. There is no alternative.

MOWBRAY.
Myself I throw, dread sovereign, at thy foot;
My life thou shalt command, but not my shame:
The one my duty owes; but my fair name,
Despite of death, that lives upon my grave
To dark dishonour's use thou shalt not have.
I am disgrac'd, impeach'd, and baffl'd here;
Pierc'd to the soul with slander's venom'd spear,
The which no balm can cure but his heart-blood
Which breath'd this poison.

I throw myself, great King, at your feet; you have command of my life, but not my honour: my duty owes you my life; but my honourable name, that will live upon my grave after I'm dead, I will not let you have for dishonour. I have been disgraced, accused and dishonoured here, stabbed to the soul with the poisonous spear of slander, and nothing can make this good except for the lifeblood of the one who slandered me.

KING RICHARD.
Rage must be withstood:
Give me his gage-lions make leopards tame.

You must overcome your anger: give me his glove–lions rule over leopards.

MOWBRAY.
Yea, but not change his spots. Take but my shame,
And I resign my gage. My dear dear lord,
The purest treasure mortal times afford
Is spotless reputation; that away,
Men are but gilded loam or painted clay.
A jewel in a ten-times barr'd-up chest
Is a bold spirit in a loyal breast.
Mine honour is my life; both grow in one;
Take honour from me, and my life is done:
Then, dear my liege, mine honour let me try;
In that I live, and for that will I die.

Yes, but they can't change his spots. Take away my dishonour, and I will give up my glove. My dear dear lord, the purest treasure that we have in our life on Earth is a spotless reputation; take that away, and men are just gilded soil or painted clay. A good spirit in a loyal heart is worth More than the most precious jewel. My honour is my life; they are intertwined; if you take my honour from me, my life is ended: so, my dear lord, let me test my honour; I live for it, and I will die for it.

KING RICHARD.
Cousin, throw up your gage; do you begin.

Cousin, throw me your glove, you start.

BOLINGBROKE.
O, God defend my soul from such deep sin!
Shall I seem crest-fallen in my father's sight?
Or with pale beggar-fear impeach my height
Before this outdar'd dastard? Ere my tongue
Shall wound my honour with such feeble wrong
Or sound so base a parle, my teeth shall tear
The slavish motive of recanting fear,
And spit it bleeding in his high disgrace,
Where shame doth harbour, even in Mowbray's face.

May God defend me against committing such a terrible sin! Should I surrender in sight of my father? Or discredit my noble birth out of cowardice in front of this cowardly bastard? Before my tongue wounds my honour with such a pathetic insult or agrees to such a dishonourable truce, my teeth shall tear it out as a punishment for its cowardice and spit it bleeding in disgrace into the place were dishonour is hiding, Mowbray's face.

Exit GAUNT

KING RICHARD.
We were not born to sue, but to command;
Which since we cannot do to make you friends,
Be ready, as your lives shall answer it,
At Coventry, upon Saint Lambert's day.
There shall your swords and lances arbitrate
The swelling difference of your settled hate;
Since we can not atone you, we shall see
Justice design the victor's chivalry.
Lord Marshal, command our officers-at-arms
Be ready to direct these home alarms.

I was not born to ask, but to order; since I can't make you be friendly, be ready, on pain of death, to appear at Coventry, upon St Lambert's day. There your swords and lances will decide this hateful argument between you; since I can't reconcile you, I shall see justice decide who will win the knightly combat. Lord Marshal, order our officers-at-arms to prepare matters for this domestic battle.

Exeunt

SCENE II.

London. The DUKE OF LANCASTER'S palace

Enter JOHN OF GAUNT with the DUCHESS OF GLOUCESTER

GAUNT.
Alas, the part I had in Woodstock's blood
Doth more solicit me than your exclaims
To stir against the butchers of his life!
But since correction lieth in those hands
Which made the fault that we cannot correct,
Put we our quarrel to the will of heaven;
Who, when they see the hours ripe on earth,
Will rain hot vengeance on offenders' heads.

Alas, my blood relationship to Woodstock is a greater motive for me than your urgings to take action against his murderers! But since punishment lies in the hands of the one who ordered the crime, we must leave judgment to the will of heaven, which, when it sees the time is right, will rain hot punishment down upon the offenders.

DUCHESS.
Finds brotherhood in thee no sharper spur?
Hath love in thy old blood no living fire?
Edward's seven sons, whereof thyself art one,
Were as seven vials of his sacred blood,
Or seven fair branches springing from one root.
Some of those seven are dried by nature's course,
Some of those branches by the Destinies cut;
But Thomas, my dear lord, my life, my Gloucester,
One vial full of Edward's sacred blood,
One flourishing branch of his most royal root,
Is crack'd, and all the precious liquor spilt;
Is hack'd down, and his summer leaves all faded,
By envy's hand and murder's bloody axe.
Ah, Gaunt, his blood was thine! That bed, that womb,
That mettle, that self mould, that fashion'd thee,
Made him a man; and though thou livest and breathest,
Yet art thou slain in him. Thou dost consent
In some large measure to thy father's death
In that thou seest thy wretched brother die,
Who was the model of thy father's life.
Call it not patience, Gaunt-it is despair;
In suff'ring thus thy brother to be slaught'red,
Thou showest the naked pathway to thy life,
Teaching stern murder how to butcher thee.

Doesn't the fact that he was your brother spur you on? Doesn't any love burn in your old blood? Edward's seven sons, of whom you are one, were like seven vials of his holy blood, or seven sweet branches springing from the same root. Some of those seven have dried up through the course of nature, some of those branches have been cut by destiny; but Thomas my dear Lord, my life, my Gloucester, one vial full of Edward's sacred blood, a flourishing branch from his royal root, has been cracked, and all the precious liquor has been spilt, chopped down, his summer leaves are all faded, by the hand of envy, and the bloody axe of a murderer. Ah, Gaunt, his blood was yours! You were made in the same bed, the same womb, from the same material, in the same mould; and though you are living and breathing, you are killed with him; you are playing a large part in your father's death if you stand by and watch your wretched brother die, who was the image of your

14

That which in mean men we entitle patience
Is pale cold cowardice in noble breasts.
What shall I say? To safeguard thine own life
The best way is to venge my Gloucester's death.

father. This is not patience, Gaunt, it is despair; in allowing your brother to be killed like this you are opening the doorway to your own murder, showing how you can be butchered too. What we call patience in lowborn men is pale cold cowardice in the hearts of the noble. What can I say? The best way to protect your own life is to take revenge for my husband's death.

GAUNT.
God's is the quarrel; for God's substitute,
His deputy anointed in His sight,
Hath caus'd his death; the which if wrongfully,
Let heaven revenge; for I may never lift
An angry arm against His minister.

The argument is with God; because God's representative, his deputy, chosen by him, caused his death; if it was wrong to do so, let God take revenge; I can never attack the minister of God.

DUCHESS.
Where then, alas, may I complain myself?

Alas, then where can I address my complaints?

GAUNT.
To God, the widow's champion and defence.

Address them to God, the defender and champion of widows.

DUCHESS.
Why then, I will. Farewell, old Gaunt.
Thou goest to Coventry, there to behold
Our cousin Hereford and fell Mowbray fight.
O, sit my husband's wrongs on Hereford's spear,
That it may enter butcher Mowbray's breast!
Or, if misfortune miss the first career,
Be Mowbray's sins so heavy in his bosom
That they may break his foaming courser's back
And throw the rider headlong in the lists,
A caitiff recreant to my cousin Hereford!
Farewell, old Gaunt; thy sometimes brother's wife,
With her companion, Grief, must end her life.

Alright, I will. Farewell, old Gaunt. You are going to Coventry, to see our cousin Hereford and evil Mowbray fight. May my husband's wrongs give power to Hereford's spear, so that it can pierce the breast of the butcher Mowbray! Or, if he is unlucky enough to miss on his first charge, may Mowbray's sins lie so heavily upon him that the weight breaks the back of his foaming charger, and throws the rider headfirst to the ground, a helpless coward at the mercy of my cousin Hereford! Farewell, old Gaunt; I was once your brother's wife, now I must live out my life with grief as my companion.

GAUNT.

Sister, farewell; I must to Coventry.
As much good stay with thee as go with me!

DUCHESS.
Yet one word more- grief boundeth where it falls,
Not with the empty hollowness, but weight.
I take my leave before I have begun,
For sorrow ends not when it seemeth done.
Commend me to thy brother, Edmund York.
Lo, this is all- nay, yet depart not so;
Though this be all, do not so quickly go;
I shall remember more. Bid him- ah, what?-
With all good speed at Plashy visit me.
Alack, and what shall good old York there see
But empty lodgings and unfurnish'd walls,
Unpeopled offices, untrodden stones?
And what hear there for welcome but my groans?
Therefore commend me; let him not come there
To seek out sorrow that dwells every where.
Desolate, desolate, will I hence and die;
The last leave of thee takes my weeping eye.

Sister, farewell; I must go to Coventry.
May as much good stay with you as goes with me!

Just one more word–grief bounces when it falls, not through its empty hollowness, but because of its weight. I'm leaving before I have begun, for sorrow is not over just because it seems to be. Remember me to your brother Edmund York. That's all–no, don't go like that, though this is all, don't go so quickly; I'll remember other things. Tell him–ah, what?– To come and see me at Plashy as soon as he can. Alas, and what shall good old York see there apart from empty rooms and bare walls, servants' quarters without servants, untrodden floors? What welcome will he hear there except for my groans? So remember him to me; don't let him go to that place that is so full of sorrow. I will go there all alone, and all alone I shall die; this is the last time my weeping eyes shall see you.

Exeunt

SCENE III.

The lists at Coventry

Enter the LORD MARSHAL and the DUKE OF AUMERLE

MARSHAL.
My Lord Aumerle, is Harry Hereford arm'd?

My Lord Aumerle, is Harry Hereford armed?

AUMERLE.
Yea, at all points; and longs to enter in.

Yes, fully; he's eager to get started.

MARSHAL.
The Duke of Norfolk, sprightfully and bold,
Stays but the summons of the appelant's trumpet.

The Duke of Norfolk, lively and brave, is just waiting for the summons of the trumpet.

AUMERLE.
Why then, the champions are prepar'd, and stay
For nothing but his Majesty's approach.

Well then, the fighters are ready, we just need to wait for the arrival of his Majesty.

The trumpets sound, and the KING enters with his nobles,
GAUNT, BUSHY, BAGOT, GREEN, and others. When they are set,
enter MOWBRAY, Duke of Nor folk, in arms, defendant, and
a HERALD

KING RICHARD.
Marshal, demand of yonder champion
The cause of his arrival here in arms;
Ask him his name; and orderly proceed
To swear him in the justice of his cause.

Marshal, ask that knight over there why he has come here armoured; ask him his name; and according to the rules ask him to swear that his cause is just.

MARSHAL.
In God's name and the King's, say who thou art,
And why thou comest thus knightly clad in arms;
Against what man thou com'st, and what thy quarrel.
Speak truly on thy knighthood and thy oath;
As so defend thee heaven and thy valour!

In the name of God and the King, say who you are, and why you have come here armoured as a knight; say who you have come to fight, and what your quarrel is with him. Speak truthfully for your knighthood and your oath; and so may heaven and your bravery defend you!

MOWBRAY.
My name is Thomas Mowbray, Duke of Norfolk;
Who hither come engaged by my oath-
Which God defend a knight should violate!-
Both to defend my loyalty and truth
To God, my King, and my succeeding issue,
Against the Duke of Hereford that appeals me;
And, by the grace of God and this mine arm,
To prove him, in defending of myself,
A traitor to my God, my King, and me.
And as I truly fight, defend me heaven!

My name is Thomas Mowbray, Duke of Norfolk; I have come here to fulfil the oath I swore– May God never let a knight break his oath!– To show both my loyalty and my honesty to God, my King, and my descendants, against the Duke of Hereford who accuses me; and, by the grace of God and with the help of my strength, to show him, in defending myself, to be a traitor to my God, my king, and to me. And as I am fighting for truth, may heaven defend me!

The trumpets sound. Enter BOLINGBROKE, Duke of Hereford,
appellant, in armour, and a HERALD

KING RICHARD.
Marshal, ask yonder knight in arms,
Both who he is and why he cometh hither
Thus plated in habiliments of war;
And formally, according to our law,
Depose him in the justice of his cause.

Marshal, asked that armoured knight who he is and why he has come here dressed ready for war; and, according to the law, make him swear to the justice of his cause.

MARSHAL.
What is thy name? and wherefore com'st thou hither
Before King Richard in his royal lists?
Against whom comest thou? and what's thy quarrel?
Speak like a true knight, so defend thee heaven!

What is your name? And why have you come here before King Richard in his royal jousting field? Who have you come to fight? What's your quarrel? Speak like a true knight, and may heaven help you!

BOLINGBROKE.
Harry of Hereford, Lancaster, and Derby,
Am I; who ready here do stand in arms
To prove, by God's grace and my body's valour,
In lists on Thomas Mowbray, Duke of Norfolk,
That he is a traitor, foul and dangerous,
To God of heaven, King Richard, and to me.
And as I truly fight, defend me heaven!

I am Harry of Hereford, Lancaster, and Derby; I have come here with my armour to prove, by the grace of God and my own bravery, by fighting Thomas Mowbray, Duke of Norfolk, that he is a traitor, foul and dangerous to the God of heaven, King Richard, and to me. And as I am fighting for truth, may heaven defend me!

MARSHAL.
On pain of death, no person be so bold
Or daring-hardy as to touch the lists,
Except the Marshal and such officers

Let no person, on pain of death, be so bold or foolhardy as to interfere with the proceedings, except for the Marshal and

Appointed to direct these fair designs.

BOLINGBROKE.
Lord Marshal, let me kiss my sovereign's hand,
And bow my knee before his Majesty;
For Mowbray and myself are like two men
That vow a long and weary pilgrimage.
Then let us take a ceremonious leave
And loving farewell of our several friends.

MARSHAL.
The appellant in all duty greets your Highness,
And craves to kiss your hand and take his leave.

KING RICHARD.
We will descend and fold him in our arms.
Cousin of Hereford, as thy cause is right,
So be thy fortune in this royal fight!
Farewell, my blood; which if to-day thou shed,
Lament we may, but not revenge thee dead.

BOLINGBROKE.
O, let no noble eye profane a tear
For me, if I be gor'd with Mowbray's spear.
As confident as is the falcon's flight
Against a bird, do I with Mowbray fight.
My loving lord, I take my leave of you;
Of you, my noble cousin, Lord Aumerle;
Not sick, although I have to do with death,
But lusty, young, and cheerly drawing breath.
Lo, as at English feasts, so I regreet
The daintiest last, to make the end most sweet.
O thou, the earthly author of my blood,
Whose youthful spirit, in me regenerate,
Doth with a twofold vigour lift me up
To reach at victory above my head,
Add proof unto mine armour with thy prayers,
And with thy blessings steel my lance's point,
That it may enter Mowbray's waxen coat
And furbish new the name of John o' Gaunt,
Even in the lusty haviour of his son.

the officers appointed to run this affair.

Lord Marshal, let me kiss the hand of my king, and kneel before his Majesty; Mowbray and myself are like two men who have sworn to go on a long and tiring pilgrimage. So let us have a formal leavetaking and bid a loving farewell to all our friends.

The plaintiff pays his respects to your Highness, and asks if he can kiss your hand and bid you farewell.

I shall come down and embrace him. My cousin Hereford, may you have whatever fortune your cause deserves in this royal fight! Farewell, relative; if you spill your blood today, we may grieve for it, but we cannot take revenge.

Oh, let no noble eye shed any tears for me, if I am wounded by Mowbray's spear! In this fight against Mowbray I am as confident as a falcon when it attacks a bird. My loving lord, I bid you farewell; the same to you, my noble cousin, Lord Aumerle; I am not sick, although I am facing death, I am lusty, young, and happy. Now, as in English banquets, I shall take the sweetest thing last, to make the end sweetest. Oh you, the procreator of my blood, whose youthful spirits reborn in me lift me up with a double strength to reach for a victory that would otherwise be unattainable, strengthen my armour with your prayers, and reinforce the point of my lance with your blessings, so it can go through Mowbray's armour as if it were wax, and let the brave achievements of his son give new honour to the name of John of Gaunt.

GAUNT.
God in thy good cause make thee prosperous!
Be swift like lightning in the execution,
And let thy blows, doubly redoubled,
Fall like amazing thunder on the casque
Of thy adverse pernicious enemy.
Rouse up thy youthful blood, be valiant, and live.

May God give you success in your noble cause! May your efforts be as swift as lightning, and let your blows, raining down, fall like stunning thunder on the helmet of your malign opposed enemy. Summon up your young courage, be brave, and live.

BOLINGBROKE.
Mine innocence and Saint George to thrive!

My innocence and St George will let me live!

MOWBRAY.
However God or fortune cast my lot,
There lives or dies, true to King Richard's throne,
A loyal, just, and upright gentleman.
Never did captive with a freer heart
Cast off his chains of bondage, and embrace
His golden uncontroll'd enfranchisement,
More than my dancing soul doth celebrate
This feast of battle with mine adversary.
Most mighty liege, and my companion peers,
Take from my mouth the wish of happy years.
As gentle and as jocund as to jest
Go I to fight: truth hath a quiet breast.

Whatever God or fortune give to me, living or dying I am true to King Richard, a loyal, just and upright gentleman. No slave was ever happier to throw off the chains of slavery, and embrace his golden freedom, than my dancing soul is happy to begin this combat with my enemy. You great King, and my fellow peers, accept my wishes for a long and happy life. I'm going into battle as peacefully and happy as if to a dance: truth gives me a quiet mind.

KING RICHARD.
Farewell, my lord, securely I espy
Virtue with valour couched in thine eye.
Order the trial, Marshal, and begin.

Farewell, my lord, I can see bravery and virtue firmly fixed in your looks. Order the combat to begin, Marshal.

MARSHAL.
Harry of Hereford, Lancaster, and Derby,
Receive thy lance; and God defend the right!

Harry of Hereford, Lancaster, and Derby, take your lance; and may God defend the just!

BOLINGBROKE.
Strong as a tower in hope, I cry amen.

My faith that this will happen is strong as a castle, I second you.

MARSHAL.
[To an officer] Go bear this lance to Thomas,
Duke of Norfolk.

Go and take this lance to Thomas, Duke of Norfolk.

FIRST HERALD.
Harry of Hereford, Lancaster, and Derby,
Stands here for God, his sovereign, and himself,
On pain to be found false and recreant,
To prove the Duke of Norfolk, Thomas Mowbray,
A traitor to his God, his King, and him;
And dares him to set forward to the fight.

Harry of Hereford, Lancaster, and Derby, stands here representing his God, his king, and himself, on penalty of being shown to be false and blasphemous, to prove that the Duke of Norfolk, Thomas Mowbray, is a traitor to his God, his king, and him; and he challenges him to step up for the fight.

SECOND HERALD.
Here standeth Thomas Mowbray, Duke of Norfolk,
On pain to be found false and recreant,
Both to defend himself, and to approve
Henry of Hereford, Lancaster, and Derby,
To God, his sovereign, and to him disloyal,
Courageously and with a free desire
Attending but the signal to begin.

Here stands Thomas Mowbray, Duke of Norfolk, on penalty of being shown to be blasphemous and false, both to defend himself, and to prove that Henry of Hereford, Lancaster, and Derby, is disloyal to God, his king, and to himself, he is waiting courageously and with free will for the signal for the combat to begin.

MARSHAL.
Sound trumpets; and set forward, combatants.
[A charge sounded]
Stay, the King hath thrown his warder down.

*Sound the trumpets; advance, combatants.
[A charge is sounded]
Wait, the King has thrown down his baton.*

KING RICHARD.
Let them lay by their helmets and their spears,
And both return back to their chairs again.
Withdraw with us; and let the trumpets sound
While we return these dukes what we decree.

Let them both put aside their helmets and their spears, and come back to their chairs. Gather round me, and let the trumpets sound, while I inform these dukes what I have decided.

A long flourish, while the KING consults his Council

Draw near,
And list what with our council we have done.
For that our kingdom's earth should not be soil'd
With that dear blood which it hath fostered;
And for our eyes do hate the dire aspect
Of civil wounds plough'd up with neighbours' sword;
And for we think the eagle-winged pride
Of sky-aspiring and ambitious thoughts,
With rival-hating envy, set on you
To wake our peace, which in our country's cradle
Draws the sweet infant breath of gentle sleep;

Come close, and listen to my decision. Because the earth of our kingdom should not be stained with the sweet blood of those who grew from it; and because my eyes hate the horrible sight of wounds cut with a neighbour's sword, and because we believe that it was pride, ambitious thoughts reaching up to the sky, causing envy of your rivals, which started you disturbing the peace, which in this sweet

Which so rous'd up with boist'rous untun'd drums,
With harsh-resounding trumpets' dreadful bray,
And grating shock of wrathful iron arms,
Might from our quiet confines fright fair peace
And make us wade even in our kindred's blood-
Therefore we banish you our territories.
You, cousin Hereford, upon pain of life,
Till twice five summers have enrich'd our fields
Shall not regreet our fair dominions,
But tread the stranger paths of banishment.

BOLINGBROKE.
Your will be done. Limit must my comfort be-
That sun that warms you here shall shine on me,
And those his golden beams to you here lent
Shall point on me and gild my banishment.

KING RICHARD.
Norfolk, for thee remains a heavier doom,
Which I with some unwillingness pronounce:
The sly slow hours shall not determinate
The dateless limit of thy dear exile;
The hopeless word of 'never to return'
Breathe I against thee, upon pain of life.

MOWBRAY.
A heavy sentence, my most sovereign liege,
And all unlook'd for from your Highness' mouth.
A dearer merit, not so deep a maim
As to be cast forth in the common air,
Have I deserved at your Highness' hands.
The language I have learnt these forty years,
My native English, now I must forgo;
And now my tongue's use is to me no more
Than an unstringed viol or a harp;
Or like a cunning instrument cas'd up
Or, being open, put into his hands
That knows no touch to tune the harmony.
Within my mouth you have engaol'd my tongue,
Doubly portcullis'd with my teeth and lips;
And dull, unfeeling, barren ignorance

country is like the breath of a sleeping baby; this is what got the war drums beating, which started the horrible discordant wail of the trumpets, and the clashing racket of iron weapons wielded in anger, which could drive beautiful peace away from our kingdom and make us have to wade through the blood of our kindred– so we exile you from our lands. You, cousin Hereford, on pain of death, will not come back into our fair lands until ten years have passed, you must live abroad as an exile.

Your will be done. I must take comfort from the fact that the sun that warms you here will shine on me, and the golden beams that are lent to you here will also fall on me and sweeten my exile.

Norfolk, you get a heavier sentence, which I pass with some regret: time will not measure the limitless period of your exile; I give you the hopeless sentence of being permanently exiled, on pain of death.

A heavy sentence, my most royal lord, and one I didn't expect to hear from your Highness. I deserved a better reward, not such a great injury from the hands of your Highness as to be sent away into the world. The language I have learnt for the past forty years, my native English, I must now forget; now my tongue is no more use to me than a violin or a heart that has no strings; or like a lovely instrument in its case–or if it is out that is placed in the Hands of one who doesn't know how to tune it or play it. You have made my tongue a prisoner in my mouth, fenced in twice by my teeth and lips, and my dull

22

Is made my gaoler to attend on me.
I am too old to fawn upon a nurse,
Too far in years to be a pupil now.
What is thy sentence, then, but speechless death,
Which robs my tongue from breathing native breath?

and empty ignorance becomes my jailer. I am too old to learn from a nanny, too far gone in years to be a pupil now: so what is your sentence but a speechless death, which robs my tongue of its right to speak its native language?

KING RICHARD.
It boots thee not to be compassionate;
After our sentence plaining comes too late.

Feeling sorry for yourself will not help you; sentence has been passed, it's too late to complain.

MOWBRAY.
Then thus I turn me from my countrv's light,
To dwell in solemn shades of endless night.

Then I will turn away from my country's light, to go and live in the darkness for ever.

KING RICHARD.
Return again, and take an oath with thee.
Lay on our royal sword your banish'd hands;
Swear by the duty that you owe to God,
Our part therein we banish with yourselves,
To keep the oath that we administer:
You never shall, so help you truth and God,
Embrace each other's love in banishment;
Nor never look upon each other's face;
Nor never write, regreet, nor reconcile
This louring tempest of your home-bred hate;
Nor never by advised purpose meet
To plot, contrive, or complot any ill,
'Gainst us, our state, our subjects, or our land.

Come back, and make an oath to go with you. Put your exiled hands on my royal sword; swear by the duty that you owe to God (the duty you owe me disappears with your exile) to keep the oath we place on you: you must swear by God and truth that you will never come together in your exile; you must never see each other; you must not write to each other; never greet each other again, you must never join your hatreds together; never arrange to meet to construct any plots against me, my office, my subjects or my country.

BOLINGBROKE.
I swear.

I swear.

MOWBRAY.
And I, to keep all this.

And so do I, I shall keep to this.

BOLINGBROKE.
Norfolk, so far as to mine enemy.
By this time, had the King permitted us,
One of our souls had wand'red in the air,
Banish'd this frail sepulchre of our flesh,
As now our flesh is banish'd from this land-
Confess thy treasons ere thou fly the realm;
Since thou hast far to go, bear not along

Norfolk, I address you though you are still my enemy. If the king had allowed it, by this time one of our souls would be wandering in the air, exiled from the weak tomb of our flesh, in the same way as our flesh is exiled from this land– confess your treason before you flee the country; since

The clogging burden of a guilty soul.

you have a long journey, do not take with you the heavy burden of a guilty soul.

MOWBRAY.
No, Bolingbroke; if ever I were traitor,
My name be blotted from the book of life,
And I from heaven banish'd as from hence!
But what thou art, God, thou, and I, do know;
And all too soon, I fear, the King shall rue.
Farewell, my liege. Now no way can I stray:
Save back to England, an the world's my way.

No, Bolingbroke; if I was ever traitor, may my name be blotted out of the book of life, and let me be exiled from heaven as I am exiled from here! But God, you, and I all know what you are; and I'm afraid the King will regret this all too soon. Farewell, my lord. I can never go astray now, unless I come back to England, I can walk wherever in the world I like.

Exit

KING RICHARD.
Uncle, even in the glasses of thine eyes
I see thy grieved heart. Thy sad aspect
Hath from the number of his banish'd years
Pluck'd four away. [To BOLINGBROKE] Six frozen
 winters spent,
Return with welcome home from banishment.

Uncle, I can see the grief in your heart in the glistening of your eyes. Your sad face takes four years off the term of his exile.[To Bolingbroke] When six cold winters have passed, you will be welcomed home from your banishment.

BOLINGBROKE.
How long a time lies in one little word!
Four lagging winters and four wanton springs
End in a word: such is the breath of Kings.

What a great period can be spanned with one word! Four slow winters and four lusty springs vanish with a word: this is the power of kings.

GAUNT.
I thank my liege that in regard of me
He shortens four years of my son's exile;
But little vantage shall I reap thereby,
For ere the six years that he hath to spend
Can change their moons and bring their times about,
My oil-dried lamp and time-bewasted light
Shall be extinct with age and endless night;
My inch of taper will be burnt and done,
And blindfold death not let me see my son.

I thank my lord that he has shortened my son's exile by four years on my account; but I shall gain little advantage from that, for before the six years that he is sentenced to are up, my ancient light will have been extinguished by time; my candle will have burnt out, andthe blindness of death will stop me from seeing my son.

KING RICHARD.
Why, uncle, thou hast many years to live.

Why, uncle, you have many years left to live.

GAUNT.
But not a minute, King, that thou canst give:
Shorten my days thou canst with sullen sorrow
And pluck nights from me, but not lend a morrow;
Thou can'st help time to furrow me with age,
But stop no wrinkle in his pilgrimage;
Thy word is current with him for my death,
But dead, thy kingdom cannot buy my breath.

But, King, you cannot give me an extra minute; you can shorten my days with miserable sadness, and take nights away from me, but you cannot add a day; you can help time to line my face with wrinkles, but you can't stop a single one of them growing; your words can easily buy my death, but your whole kingdom can't buy my life back once I'm dead.

KING RICHARD.
Thy son is banish'd upon good advice,
Whereto thy tongue a party-verdict gave.
Why at our justice seem'st thou then to lour?

Your son is exiled on wise advice, to which you agreed. Why does our sentence now seem so bad?

GAUNT.
Things sweet to taste prove in digestion sour.
You urg'd me as a judge; but I had rather
You would have bid me argue like a father.
O, had it been a stranger, not my child,
To smooth his fault I should have been more mild.
A partial slander sought I to avoid,
And in the sentence my own life destroy'd.
Alas, I look'd when some of you should say
I was too strict to make mine own away;
But you gave leave to my unwilling tongue
Against my will to do myself this wrong.

Things which taste sweet can often upset the digestion. You asked me to rule as a judge; I would rather that you asked me to argue as a father. Oh, if it had been a stranger, not my child, I would not have punished him so harshly. I wanted to avoid accusations of bias, and by doing so destroyed my own life. Alas, I hoped that some of you would say that I was being too strict in exiling my own son; but you allowed my unwilling tongue to commit this harm against myself.

KING RICHARD.
Cousin, farewell; and, uncle, bid him so.
Six years we banish him, and he shall go.

Cousin, farewell; and, uncle, say the same to him. I have banished him for six years, and he shall go.

Flourish. Exit KING with train

AUMERLE.
Cousin, farewell; what presence must not know,
From where you do remain let paper show.

Cousin, farewell; what I can't hear from your own mouth, let me know in your letters.

MARSHAL.
My lord, no leave take I, for I will ride
As far as land will let me by your side.

My lord, I won't say goodbye, for I will ride with you to the frontiers of the

GAUNT.
O, to what purpose dost thou hoard thy words,
That thou returnest no greeting to thy friends?

BOLINGBROKE.
I have too few to take my leave of you,
When the tongue's office should be prodigal
To breathe the abundant dolour of the heart.

GAUNT.
Thy grief is but thy absence for a time.

BOLINGBROKE.
Joy absent, grief is present for that time.

GAUNT.
What is six winters? They are quickly gone.

BOLINGBROKE.
To men in joy; but grief makes one hour ten.

GAUNT.
Call it a travel that thou tak'st for pleasure.

BOLINGBROKE.
My heart will sigh when I miscall it so,
Which finds it an enforced pilgrimage.

GAUNT.
The sullen passage of thy weary steps
Esteem as foil wherein thou art to set
The precious jewel of thy home return.

BOLINGBROKE.
Nay, rather, every tedious stride I make
Will but remember me what a deal of world
I wander from the jewels that I love.
Must I not serve a long apprenticehood

kingdom.

*Why are you saving your words,
not answering your friends?*

*I have too few words to say goodbye,
my tongue is not rich enough to show
the wealth of grief that is in my heart.*

*Your sadness is only at your exile for a
time.*

*For all that time joy will be absent, grief
present.*

*What are six winters? They will pass
quickly.*

*For happy men; sorrow makes every hour
seem like ten.*

*Think of it as a holiday you are taking for
pleasure.*

*If I misdescribed it like that my heart
would sigh, it thinks of this as an enforced
pilgrimage.*

*Think of your weary dull journey as
a setting in which you will place
the precious jewel of your return home.*

*No, it's more like every tedious step I take
will remind me how far I am travelling
away from the jewels that I love.
I am condemned to spending years*

To foreign passages; and in the end,
Having my freedom, boast of nothing else
But that I was a journeyman to grief?

GAUNT.
All places that the eye of heaven visits
Are to a wise man ports and happy havens.
Teach thy necessity to reason thus:
There is no virtue like necessity.
Think not the King did banish thee,
But thou the King. Woe doth the heavier sit
Where it perceives it is but faintly borne.
Go, say I sent thee forth to purchase honour,
And not the King exil'd thee; or suppose
Devouring pestilence hangs in our air
And thou art flying to a fresher clime.
Look what thy soul holds dear, imagine it
To lie that way thou goest, not whence thou com'st.
Suppose the singing birds musicians,
The grass whereon thou tread'st the presence strew'd,
The flowers fair ladies, and thy steps no more
Than a delightful measure or a dance;
For gnarling sorrow hath less power to bite
The man that mocks at it and sets it light.

BOLINGBROKE.
O, who can hold a fire in his hand
By thinking on the frosty Caucasus?
Or cloy the hungry edge of appetite
By bare imagination of a feast?
Or wallow naked in December snow
By thinking on fantastic summer's heat?
O, no! the apprehension of the good
Gives but the greater feeling to the worse.
Fell sorrow's tooth doth never rankle more
Than when he bites, but lanceth not the sore.

GAUNT.
Come, come, my son, I'll bring thee on thy way.
Had I thy youth and cause, I would not stay.

BOLINGBROKE.

*wandering abroad; and in the end,
when I regain my freedom, all I shall have
when I come home is sorrow.*

*Every place the sun shines on
is a happy one and a good shelter for the
wise man. You must learn to think like
this: necessity creates its own virtues.
Don't think that the King has exiled you,
but that you have exiled the king. Sorrow
is greater when you do not face it
courageously. Go, say I sent you away to
seek your fortune, and not that the King
banished you; or pretend that there is a
fatal plague in our air and that you are
fleeing to a more healthy climate. Think of
what is dearest to you, and imagine that
you are journeying towards it, not away
from it. Imagine that the singing birds
are musicians, the grass you walk on the
carpet of the royal chamber, the flowers
fair ladies, and your steps are no more
than a delightful dance;
snarling sorrow has less power to harm
the man who mocks it and doesn't care.*

*Oh, who can keep warm
by thinking of the frosty Caucasus?
Who can take the edge off his hunger
by imagining a feast?
Who can run naked through the snow of
December by imagining the heat of
summer? Oh no, remembering good things
just makes the bad things seem worse.
The bite of sorrow it is at its worst
when it just breaks the skin, to make a
festering sore.*

*Come, come, my son, I'll go with you on
your way. If I had your youth and cause,
I would not stay.*

Then, England's ground, farewell; sweet soil, adieu;
My mother, and my nurse, that bears me yet!
Where'er I wander, boast of this I can:
Though banish'd, yet a trueborn English man.

So, farewell to the land of England; sweet soil, goodbye; my mother, and my nurse, that still carries me! Wherever I wonder, I can boast of this: although I am exiled, I am still a true born English man.

Exeunt

SCENE IV.

London. The court

Enter the KING, with BAGOT and GREEN, at one door;
and the DUKE OF AUMERLE at another

KING RICHARD.
We did observe. Cousin Aumerle,
How far brought you high Hereford on his way?

*It was noted. Cousin Aumerle,
how far did you accompany high
Hereford?*

AUMERLE.
I brought high Hereford, if you call him so,
But to the next high way, and there I left him.

*I took high Hereford, if that's what you
call him, just to the next highway, and left
him there.*

KING RICHARD.
And say, what store of parting tears were shed?

*And tell me, how many tears were shed
when you parted?*

AUMERLE.
Faith, none for me; except the north-east wind,
Which then blew bitterly against our faces,
Awak'd the sleeping rheum, and so by chance
Did grace our hollow parting with a tear.

*I swear, none for me; except that the
north-east wind, which was blowing
bitterly in our faces, made our eyes water,
and so perhaps that caused a tear at our
empty farewell.*

KING RICHARD.
What said our cousin when you parted with him?

*What did my cousin say when you left
him?*

AUMERLE.
'Farewell.'
And, for my heart disdained that my tongue
Should so profane the word, that taught me craft
To counterfeit oppression of such grief
That words seem'd buried in my sorrow's grave.
Marry, would the word 'farewell' have length'ned hours
And added years to his short banishment,
He should have had a volume of farewells;
But since it would not, he had none of me.

*'Farewell.'
And, as I didn't want to be so false
as to use the word, I pretended
that I was so overwhelmed with grief
that I was unable to speak.
Indeed, if the word 'farewell' could have
extended time and added years to his short
exile, I would have given him a thousand
farewells; but since it wouldn't, he got*

29

none from me.

KING RICHARD.
He is our cousin, cousin; but 'tis doubt,
When time shall call him home from banishment,
Whether our kinsman come to see his friends.
Ourself, and Bushy, Bagot here, and Green,
Observ'd his courtship to the common people;
How he did seem to dive into their hearts
With humble and familiar courtesy;
What reverence he did throw away on slaves,
Wooing poor craftsmen with the craft of smiles
And patient underbearing of his fortune,
As 'twere to banish their affects with him.
Off goes his bonnet to an oyster-wench;
A brace of draymen bid God speed him well
And had the tribute of his supple knee,
With 'Thanks, my countrymen, my loving friends';
As were our England in reversion his,
And he our subjects' next degree in hope.

He is my cousin, cousin; but it's doubtful, when the period of exile has expired, if our kinsman will come to see his friends. Bushy, Bagot here, Green, and myself noticed how he courted the common people; he seemed to insinuate himself into their hearts by pretending to be humble and friendly; how he seemed to worship slaves, wooing poor craftsmen with smiles and modest endurance of his fate, as if he wanted to carry their affection into exile with him. He tipped his hat to an oyster seller; a pair of carters wished him Godspeed and he bowed the knee to them, saying, 'Thanks, my countrymen, my loving friends' – as if my England really belonged to him, and he would be the next one to rule them.

GREEN.
Well, he is gone; and with him go these thoughts!
Now for the rebels which stand out in Ireland,
Expedient manage must be made, my liege,
Ere further leisure yicld them further means
For their advantage and your Highness' loss.

Well, he is gone; let those thoughts go with him! Now, we must formulate a plan for dealing with the rebels in Ireland, my lord, any delay will give them greater opportunities to take advantage and damage your Highness.

KING RICHARD.
We will ourself in person to this war;
And, for our coffers, with too great a court
And liberal largess, are grown somewhat light,
We are enforc'd to farm our royal realm;
The revenue whereof shall furnish us
For our affairs in hand. If that come short,
Our substitutes at home shall have blank charters;
Whereto, when they shall know what men are rich,
They shall subscribe them for large sums of gold,
And send them after to supply our wants;
For we will make for Ireland presently.

I will go to this war myself in person; and as the Exchequer has become somewhat impoverished through keeping too large a court and being too generous I shall have to lease out the tax-raising rights; the income from that will give me enough to deal with the current business. If that's not enough, our stand-ins at home shall be given blank cheques, which they can make the richest men sign to provide us with large sums of gold, and they can send these on to us to supply our needs; I will go to Ireland at once.
[Enter Bushy]
Bushy, what news is there?

Enter BUSHY
Bushy, what news?

BUSHY.
Old John of Gaunt is grievous sick, my lord,
Suddenly taken; and hath sent poste-haste
To entreat your Majesty to visit him.

*Old John of Gaunt is seriously ill, my lord,
it came upon him suddenly; he has sent
urgent messages begging your Majesty to
visit him.*

KING RICHARD.
Where lies he?

Where is he?

BUSHY.
At Ely House.

At Ely House.

KING RICHARD.
Now put it, God, in the physician's mind
To help him to his grave immediately!
The lining of his coffers shall make coats
To deck our soldiers for these Irish wars.
Come, gentlemen, let's all go visit him.
Pray God we may make haste, and come too late!

*Now, God, put it in the doctor's mind
to help him straight into his grave!
The money from his estate will pay
for the equipment of our soldiers in these
Irish wars. Come, gentlemen, let's all go
and visit him. May God speed us there,
and may we be too late!*

ALL.
Amen.

Amen.

Exeunt

ACT II.

SCENE I.

London. Ely House

Enter JOHN OF GAUNT, sick, with the DUKE OF YORK, etc.

GAUNT.
Will the King come, that I may breathe my last
In wholesome counsel to his unstaid youth?

Will the King come, so I may use my last breath to give sensible advice to this hotheaded youth?

YORK.
Vex not yourself, nor strive not with your breath;
For all in vain comes counsel to his ear.

Don't trouble yourself, or fight for breath; he doesn't listen to advice.

GAUNT.
O, but they say the tongues of dying men
Enforce attention like deep harmony.
Where words are scarce, they are seldom spent in vain;
For they breathe truth that breathe their words -in pain.
He that no more must say is listen'd more
Than they whom youth and ease have taught to glose;
More are men's ends mark'd than their lives before.
The setting sun, and music at the close,
As the last taste of sweets, is sweetest last,
Writ in remembrance more than things long past.
Though Richard my life's counsel would not hear,
My death's sad tale may yet undeaf his ear.

Oh, but they say the speech of dying men holds the attention like great music. When you don't have many words, you don't waste them; those for whom it is painful to speak speak the truth. Someone whose time is running out is listened to more than someone whom youth and leisure has taught to speak smoothly; people take more note of a man's ending than his earlier life. The setting sun, the last phrase of a piece of music, the last taste of sweet things, stay sweetest the longest, stay in the memory longer than things long past. Though Richard wouldn't listen to my advice during my life, he might listen to what I have to say as I'm dying.

YORK.
No; it is stopp'd with other flattering sounds,
As praises, of whose taste the wise are fond,
Lascivious metres, to whose venom sound
The open ear of youth doth always listen;
Report of fashions in proud Italy,
Whose manners still our tardy apish nation
Limps after in base imitation.

No; his ears are blocked with other flattering voices, praises, which can make the sensible stupid, sexual verses, whose poisonous sound young men have always liked to listen to; reports of the fashions in great Italy, whose manners our backward copying nation limps after, making a poor

Where doth the world thrust forth a vanity-
So it be new, there's no respect how vile-
That is not quickly buzz'd into his ears?
Then all too late comes counsel to be heard
Where will doth mutiny with wit's regard.
Direct not him whose way himself will choose.
'Tis breath thou lack'st, and that breath wilt thou lose.

GAUNT.
Methinks I am a prophet new inspir'd,
And thus expiring do foretell of him:
His rash fierce blaze of riot cannot last,
For violent fires soon burn out themselves;
Small showers last long, but sudden storms are short;
He tires betimes that spurs too fast betimes;
With eager feeding food doth choke the feeder;
Light vanity, insatiate cormorant,
Consuming means, soon preys upon itself.
This royal throne of kings, this scept'red isle,
This earth of majesty, this seat of Mars,
This other Eden, demi-paradise,
This fortress built by Nature for herself
Against infection and the hand of war,
This happy breed of men, this little world,
This precious stone set in the silver sea,
Which serves it in the office of a wall,
Or as a moat defensive to a house,
Against the envy of less happier lands;
This blessed plot, this earth, this realm, this England,
This nurse, this teeming womb of royal kings,
Fear'd by their breed, and famous by their birth,
Renowned for their deeds as far from home,
For Christian service and true chivalry,
As is the sepulchre in stubborn Jewry
Of the world's ransom, blessed Mary's Son;
This land of such dear souls, this dear dear land,
Dear for her reputation through the world,
Is now leas'd out-I die pronouncing it-
Like to a tenement or pelting farm.
England, bound in with the triumphant sea,
Whose rocky shore beats back the envious siege
Of wat'ry Neptune, is now bound in with shame,
With inky blots and rotten parchment bonds;
That England, that was wont to conquer others,

imitation. What frivolous thing is there in the world– as long as it's new, he doesn't care how horrid– that isn't quickly brought to his attention? Then good advice comes all too late where reason is overcome by desire. Don't advise him, he does as he pleases. You are short of breath, advising him would be a waste of it.

I feel like a prophet with new inspiration, and as I die I predict this of him: his foolish angry eruption cannot last, for raging fires soon burn themselves out; it can drizzle for hours, but sudden storms are quickly over; someone who rides too fast too early will tire themselves; if you eat too fast you will choke; such vanity is like the insatiable cormorant, which once it's eaten everything starts on itself. This royal seat of Kings, this ruling land, the home of Majesty, the throne of war, this other Eden, second paradise, this fortress built by nature for herself against infection and attacks, this fortunate race of men, this little world, this precious stone set in the silver sea, which serves as a defensive wall, or like a moat around the house, against the jealousy of less happy nations; this blessed plot, this earth, this realm, this England, this nurse, this breeding ground of royal kings, feared due to their ancestry, and famous for their parentage, celebrated for their deeds in faraway lands, for Christian service and true chivalry, as they showed in their efforts in Israel, recapturing the grave of Jesus; this land of such sweet souls, this dear dear land, loved for her reputation throughout the world, is now rented out–I announce it as I die– like a field or a smallholding. England, ringed round with the victorious sea, his rocky shore beats back the jealous attacks of the ocean, is now enslaved by shame, tied up with

Hath made a shameful conquest of itself.
Ah, would the scandal vanish with my life,
How happy then were my ensuing death!

rotten inky documents; England, that used to conquer others, has shamefully conquered itself. Ah, I wish the scandal would vanish with my life, how happy I would be to die then!

Enter KING and QUEEN, AUMERLE, BUSHY, GREEN, BAGOT,
Ross, and WILLOUGHBY

YORK.
The King is come; deal mildly with his youth,
For young hot colts being rag'd do rage the more.

The King has come; treat him calmly, because rash young men answer anger with anger.

QUEEN.
How fares our noble uncle Lancaster?

How is our noble uncle Lancaster?

KING RICHARD.
What comfort, man? How is't with aged Gaunt?

What hope is there, man? How is old Gaunt?

GAUNT.
O, how that name befits my composition!
Old Gaunt, indeed; and gaunt in being old.
Within me grief hath kept a tedious fast;
And who abstains from meat that is not gaunt?
For sleeping England long time have I watch'd;
Watching breeds leanness, leanness is all gaunt.
The pleasure that some fathers feed upon
Is my strict fast-I mean my children's looks;
And therein fasting, hast thou made me gaunt.
Gaunt am I for the grave, gaunt as a grave,
Whose hollow womb inherits nought but bones.

Oh, how suited that name is to my constitution! Old Gaunt, indeed; and age has made me gaunt. Grief has kept me from eating; who can abstain from meat and not be gaunt? I have stayed awake for a long time guarding sleeping England; that makes you thin, and thinness makes you gaunt. The pleasure that some fathers feed themselves with, I abstain from—I mean looking at my children; starving me of that, you have made me gaunt. I am gaunt for the grave, gaunt as a grave, her hollow womb only accepts bones.

KING RICHARD.
Can sick men play so nicely with their names?

Can a sick man make such good wordplay with his name?

GAUNT.
No, misery makes sport to mock itself:
Since thou dost seek to kill my name in me,
I mock my name, great king, to flatter thee.

No, it's misery which enjoys mocking itself: since you have tried to end my family name, I mock it, great King, to flatter you.

KING RICHARD.
Should dying men flatter with those that live?

Should dying men flatter those who are still alive?

GAUNT.
No, no; men living flatter those that die.

No, no; living men flatter those who die.

KING RICHARD.
Thou, now a-dying, sayest thou flatterest me.

You, who are dying, say you are flattering me.

GAUNT.
O, no! thou diest, though I the sicker be.

Oh no! You are dying, although I am sicker.

KING RICHARD.
I am in health, I breathe, and see thee ill.

I am well, I'm breathing, and I see you ill.

GAUNT.
Now He that made me knows I see thee ill;
Ill in myself to see, and in thee seeing ill.
Thy death-bed is no lesser than thy land
Wherein thou liest in reputation sick;
And thou, too careless patient as thou art,
Commit'st thy anointed body to the cure
Of those physicians that first wounded thee:
A thousand flatterers sit within thy crown,
Whose compass is no bigger than thy head;
And yet, incaged in so small a verge,
The waste is no whit lesser than thy land.
O, had thy grandsire with a prophet's eye
Seen how his son's son should destroy his sons,
From forth thy reach he would have laid thy shame,
Deposing thee before thou wert possess'd,
Which art possess'd now to depose thyself.
Why, cousin, wert thou regent of the world,
It were a shame to let this land by lease;
But for thy world enjoying but this land,
Is it not more than shame to shame it so?
Landlord of England art thou now, not King.
Thy state of law is bondslave to the law;
And thou-

Now the one who made me knows I see you ill, I have ill vision and also I can see illness within you. Your deathbed is your whole country, where your reputation is sick, and you, being too careless a patient, hand your holy body over to be cured by those doctors that first wounded you: a thousand flatterers sit within your crown, whose circumference is no bigger than your head, and yet, trapped within such small boundaries, there is an evil no smaller than your whole land. Oh, if your grandfather had been a prophet and seen how his grandson would destroy his family, he would have taken your opportunities out of your reach, stopping you before you could assume the crown which you are now madly going to throw away yourself. Why, cousin, if you ruled the whole world, it would be shameful to rent out this land; but as this land is all you rule over, isn't it more shameful to put this shame on it? You are now the landlord of England, not its King, your great office is mortgaged to the law, and you—

KING RICHARD.
A lunatic lean-witted fool,
Presuming on an ague's privilege,
Darest with thy frozen admonition
Make pale our cheek, chasing the royal blood
With fury from his native residence.
Now by my seat's right royal majesty,
Wert thou not brother to great Edward's son,
This tongue that runs so roundly in thy head
Should run thy head from thy unreverent shoulders.

A crazy half witted fool, taking advantage of the privileges of the sick, who dares with your cold criticism to make me turn pale, draining the royal blood out of my face with anger. I swear by my truly royal majestic throne that if you weren't the brother of the son of great Edward this tongue which you let run so freely would become the axe which cuts off your disrespectful head.

GAUNT.
O, Spare me not, my brother Edward's son,
For that I was his father Edward's son;
That blood already, like the pelican,
Hast thou tapp'd out, and drunkenly carous'd.
My brother Gloucester, plain well-meaning soul-
Whom fair befall in heaven 'mongst happy souls!-
May be a precedent and witness good
That thou respect'st not spilling Edward's blood.
Join with the present sickness that I have;
And thy unkindness be like crooked age,
To crop at once a too long withered flower.
Live in thy shame, but die not shame with thee!
These words hereafter thy tormentors be!
Convey me to my bed, then to my grave.
Love they to live that love and honour have.

Oh, do not spare me, my brother Edward's son, just because I was his father Edward's son; you have already spilt that blood and drunkenly swilled it like a pelican. My brother Gloucester, a simple well-meaning soul, whom I hope has got a good welcome in heaven, can be a good witness to the fact that you don't care about spilling Edward's blood. Add yourself to my current illness, let your unkindness be like a scythe, chopping down at once an already dying flower. Live with your shame, but your shame won't die with you! May these words torture you forever! Carry me to my bed, then to my grave– love the ones who are living who still have love and honour.

Exit, borne out by his attendants

KING RICHARD.
And let them die that age and sullens have;
For both hast thou, and both become the grave.

And let the ones who are old and sullen die; you are both, and both are suitable for the grave.

YORK.
I do beseech your Majesty impute his words
To wayward sickliness and age in him.
He loves you, on my life, and holds you dear
As Harry Duke of Hereford, were he here.

I beg your Majesty to regard his words as the product of his illness and his age. He loves you, I swear, and you're as dear to him as Harry Duke of Hereford, if he were here.

KING RICHARD.
Right, you say true: as Hereford's love, so his;
As theirs, so mine; and all be as it is.

Right, you are right: Hereford's love is like his; mine is like theirs; that's how everything is.

Enter NORTHUMBERLAND

NORTHUMBERLAND.
My liege, old Gaunt commends him to your
Majesty.

My lord, old Gaunt sends your Majesty his compliments.

KING RICHARD.
What says he?

What does he say?

NORTHUMBERLAND.
Nay, nothing; all is said.
His tongue is now a stringless instrument;
Words, life, and all, old Lancaster hath spent.

No, nothing; all has been said. His tongue is now mute; old Lancaster has spent his words, his life and all.

YORK.
Be York the next that must be bankrupt so!
Though death be poor, it ends a mortal woe.

Let York be the next man to be so bankrupt! Though death is poor, it ends the pain of life.

KING RICHARD.
The ripest fruit first falls, and so doth he;
His time is spent, our pilgrimage must be.
So much for that. Now for our Irish wars.
We must supplant those rough rug-headed kerns,
Which live like venom where no venom else
But only they have privilege to live.
And for these great affairs do ask some charge,
Towards our assistance we do seize to us
The plate, coin, revenues, and moveables,
Whereof our uncle Gaunt did stand possess'd.

The ripest fruit falls first, and so he does; his time is up, and so is our pilgrimage. So much for that. Now for the Irish wars. We must overthrow those shaggy headed fighters, who are a poison in a place where no other apart from them is allowed to survive. As this great business must be paid for, to help us we shall take possession of the plate, money, revenues, and goods which our uncle Gaunt owned.

YORK.
How long shall I be patient? Ah, how long
Shall tender duty make me suffer wrong?
Not Gloucester's death, nor Hereford's banishment,
Nor Gaunt's rebukes, nor England's private wrongs,
Nor the prevention of poor Bolingbroke
About his marriage, nor my own disgrace,
Have ever made me sour my patient cheek
Or bend one wrinkle on my sovereign's face.

How long will I put up with this? Ah, how Long shall my sense of duty make me endure evil? Neither Gloucester's death, nor Hereford's exile, nor Gaunt's criticisms, nor England's suffering, nor the blocking of poor Bolingbroke's marriage, nor my own disgrace, have ever made me shed a tear,

I am the last of noble Edward's sons,
Of whom thy father, Prince of Wales, was first.
In war was never lion rag'd more fierce,
In peace was never gentle lamb more mild,
Than was that young and princely gentleman.
His face thou hast, for even so look'd he,
Accomplish'd with the number of thy hours;
But when he frown'd, it was against the French
And not against his friends. His noble hand
Did win what he did spend, and spent not that
Which his triumphant father's hand had won.
His hands were guilty of no kindred blood,
But bloody with the enemies of his kin.
O Richard! York is too far gone with grief,
Or else he never would compare between-

KING RICHARD.
Why, uncle, what's the matter?

YORK.
O my liege,
Pardon me, if you please; if not, I, pleas'd
Not to be pardoned, am content withal.
Seek you to seize and gripe into your hands
The royalties and rights of banish'd Hereford?
Is not Gaunt dead? and doth not Hereford live?
Was not Gaunt just? and is not Harry true?
Did not the one deserve to have an heir?
Is not his heir a well-deserving son?
Take Hereford's rights away, and take from Time
His charters and his customary rights;
Let not to-morrow then ensue to-day;
Be not thyself-for how art thou a king
But by fair sequence and succession?
Now, afore God-God forbid I say true!-
If you do wrongfully seize Hereford's rights,
Call in the letters patents that he hath
By his attorneys-general to sue
His livery, and deny his off'red homage,
You pluck a thousand dangers on your head,
You lose a thousand well-disposed hearts,
And prick my tender patience to those thoughts
Which honour and allegiance cannot think.

*or frown once in the face of my king.
I am the last son of noble Edward,
of whom your father, the Prince of Wales,
was the first. There was never a fiercer
lion in battle, never a gentler lamb in
peace, than that young and regal
gentleman. You have his face, that's how
he looked, when he was the same age as
you; when he fought it was with the
French, and not with his friends; his
noble hand only spent what he had won,
and didn't spend what his triumphant
father had won; he did not have any
family blood on his hands, they were
bloody with that of his family's enemies.
Oh Richard! York has gone mad in his
grief, otherwise he would never compare–*

Why, uncle, what's the matter?

*Oh my lord,
please excuse me; if not, I'm pleased
not to be excused, I'll be happy whatever.
Do you want to grab into your hands
the property and titles of exiled Hereford?
Isn't Gaunt dead? And isn't Hereford
alive? Wasn't Gaunt fair? Isn't Harry
good? Didn't the one deserve to have an
heir? Isn't his heir a son who deserved his
inheritance? Take Hereford's rights away,
and remove all thethings he is due by
custom from history; then don't let
tomorrow follow on from today: don't be
who you are. For how are you a king
except by the fair rules of inheritance?
Now before God–may God forbid this
happens!– If you wrongly seize Hereford's
rights, revoke the legal permission that he
has to claim his father's lands and reject
his offers of loyalty, you are calling down
a thousand dangers on your head, you
will lose a thousand well disposed hearts,
and you will make my sensitive mind think
things which honour and loyalty should*

not.

KING RICHARD.
Think what you will, we seize into our hands
His plate, his goods, his money, and his lands.

Think what you like, I am taking his plate, his goods, his money and his lands.

YORK.
I'll not be by the while. My liege, farewell.
What will ensue hereof there's none can tell;
But by bad courses may be understood
That their events can never fall out good.

I won't stand by and watch. My lord, farewell. Nobody can tell what will come of this; but we can clearly see that bad behavior never leads to a good outcome.

Exit

KING RICHARD.
Go, Bushy, to the Earl of Wiltshire straight;
Bid him repair to us to Ely House
To see this business. To-morrow next
We will for Ireland; and 'tis time, I trow.
And we create, in absence of ourself,
Our Uncle York Lord Governor of England;
For he is just, and always lov'd us well.
Come on, our queen; to-morrow must we part;
Be merry, for our time of stay is short.

Bushy, go straight to the Earl of Wiltshire; tell him to come to us at Ely House to see to this business. Tomorrow I shall go to Ireland, I think it's time. In my absence I appoint my uncle York Lord Governor of England; he is fair, and has always been good to me. Come on, my queen; tomorrow we must part; let's be jolly, for we don't have long.

Flourish. Exeunt KING, QUEEN, BUSHY, AUMERLE, GREEN, and BAGOT

NORTHUMBERLAND.
Well, lords, the Duke of Lancaster is dead.

Well, lords, the Duke of Lancaster is dead.

ROSS.
And living too; for now his son is Duke.

And living too; for his son is now Duke.

WILLOUGHBY.
Barely in title, not in revenues.

Hardly in name, not in income.

NORTHUMBERLAND.
Richly in both, if justice had her right.

If there was any justice he would be rich in both.

ROSS.
My heart is great; but it must break with silence,
Ere't be disburdened with a liberal tongue.

My heart is full; but it must remain silent, in case, speaking, it would say too much.

NORTHUMBERLAND.
Nay, speak thy mind; and let him ne'er speak
More
That speaks thy words again to do thee harm!

No, say what you're thinking; don't let anyone
repeat your words to do you harm!

WILLOUGHBY.
Tends that thou wouldst speak to the Duke of
Hereford?
If it be so, out with it boldly, man;
Quick is mine ear to hear of good towards him.

Do you have something to say about the Duke of Hereford?
If that's the case, spit it out, man;
I'm eager to hear good things about him.

ROSS.
No good at all that I can do for him;
Unless you call it good to pity him,
Bereft and gelded of his patrimony.

I can't do any good for him;
unless you think it's good to pity him,
stripped of all his inheritance.

NORTHUMBERLAND.
Now, afore God, 'tis shame such wrongs are
borne
In him, a royal prince, and many moe
Of noble blood in this declining land.
The King is not himself, but basely led
By flatterers; and what they will inform,
Merely in hate, 'gainst any of us all,
That will the King severely prosecute
'Gainst us, our lives, our children, and our heirs.

Now, I swear to God, it's shameful that such wrongs are suffered
by him, a royal prince, and many others
of his noble blood in this declining
country. The King is not himself, he is led
astray by flatterers; and what they will say
to him out of pure hate, against any of us,
will make the King launch harsh attacks
against us, our lives, our children and our heirs.

ROSS.
The commons hath he pill'd with grievous taxes;
And quite lost their hearts; the nobles hath he find
For ancient quarrels and quite lost their hearts.

He has piled exorbitant taxes on the common people; he has completely lost
their hearts; he has fined the noblemen for
ancient quarrels and lost them too.

WILLOUGHBY.
And daily new exactions are devis'd,
As blanks, benevolences, and I wot not what;
But what, a God's name, doth become of this?

And every day new taxes are invented,
blank cheques, forced loans, I don't know
what else; what in God's name will all this
lead to?

NORTHUMBERLAND.
Wars hath not wasted it, for warr'd he hath
not,
But basely yielded upon compromise
That which his noble ancestors achiev'd with blows.

It hasn't gone on wars, for he hasn't been to war,
he has cravenly won through negotiation
what his ancestors achieved with force.

More hath he spent in peace than they in wars.

He has spent more on peace than they did on war.

ROSS.
The Earl of Wiltshire hath the realm in farm.

The Earl of Wiltshire is farming the country.

WILLOUGHBY.
The King's grown bankrupt like a broken man.

The King has gone bankrupt like a ruined man.

NORTHUMBERLAND.
Reproach and dissolution hangeth over him.

Criticism and disillusionment hang over him.

ROSS.
He hath not money for these Irish wars,
His burdenous taxations notwithstanding,
But by the robbing of the banish'd Duke.

He can't afford these Irish wars, despite his excessive taxation, except by robbing the exiled Duke.

NORTHUMBERLAND.
His noble kinsman-most degenerate king!
But, lords, we hear this fearful tempest sing,
Yet seek no shelter to avoid the storm;
We see the wind sit sore upon our sails,
And yet we strike not, but securely perish.

His noble relative–what a degenerate king! But, lords, we hear this terrible storm blowing, and yet we don't try to find shelter; we see the wind about to tear down our sails, and yet we don't take them down, we die through our arrogance.

ROSS.
We see the very wreck that we must suffer;
And unavoided is the danger now
For suffering so the causes of our wreck.

We can see exactly the calamity coming to us; and the danger is now unavoidable, the crash is inevitable.

NORTHUMBERLAND.
Not so; even through the hollow eyes of death
I spy life peering; but I dare not say
How near the tidings of our comfort is.

It is not, where there's life there's still hope; but I can't say how close our rescue is.

WILLOUGHBY.
Nay, let us share thy thoughts as thou dost ours.

No, let us share your thoughts as you share ours.

ROSS.
Be confident to speak, Northumberland.
We three are but thyself, and, speaking so,

Speak with confidence, Northumberland. We three are just like you, and so speaking

Thy words are but as thoughts; therefore be bold.

NORTHUMBERLAND.
Then thus: I have from Le Port Blanc, a bay
In Brittany, receiv'd intelligence
That Harry Duke of Hereford, Rainold Lord Cobham,
That late broke from the Duke of Exeter,
His brother, Archbishop late of Canterbury,
Sir Thomas Erpingham, Sir John Ramston,
Sir John Norbery, Sir Robert Waterton, and Francis
Quoint-
All these, well furnish'd by the Duke of Britaine,
With eight tall ships, three thousand men of war,
Are making hither with all due expedience,
And shortly mean to touch our northern shore.
Perhaps they had ere this, but that they stay
The first departing of the King for Ireland.
If then we shall shake off our slavish yoke,
Imp out our drooping country's broken wing,
Redeem from broking pawn the blemish'd crown,
Wipe off the dust that hides our sceptre's gilt,
And make high majesty look like itself,
Away with me in post to Ravenspurgh;
But if you faint, as fearing to do so,
Stay and be secret, and myself will go.

ROSS.
To horse, to horse! Urge doubts to them that fear.

WILLOUGHBY.
Hold out my horse, and I will first be there.

to us is just like thinking; so speak out.

Then this is it: I have received from Port le Blanc, a bay in Brittany, news that Harry Duke of Hereford, Rainold Lord Cobham, who recently deserted the Duke of Exeter, his brother, recently Archbishop of Canterbury, Sir Thomas Erpingham, Sir John Ramston, Sir John Norbery, Sir Robert Waterton, and Francis Quoint— these men have been well equipped by the Duke of Brittany with eight warships, three thousand soldiers, who are coming here as quickly as they can, and intend to land soon on our northern shores. Maybe they would have come before, but they have been waiting for the king to leave for Ireland. If you want to throw off our slavish burdens, repair the broken wing of our limping country, take the dishonoured crown back out of pawn, wipe off the dust which is hiding the gold of the sceptre, and restore the dignity of the throne, then hurry away with me to Ravenspurgh; but if you are fainthearted and don't dare to do so, stay here, don't say anything, and I will go alone.

Get the horses! Only the fainthearted will doubt.

If my horse holds out, I'll be first there.

Exeunt

SCENE II.

Windsor Castle

Enter QUEEN, BUSHY, and BAGOT

BUSHY.
Madam, your Majesty is too much sad.
You promis'd, when you parted with the King,
To lay aside life-harming heaviness
And entertain a cheerful disposition.

Madam, your Majesty is much too sad. When you parted from the king you promised that you would set aside harmful depression and keep your spirits up.

QUEEN.
To please the King, I did; to please myself
I cannot do it; yet I know no cause
Why I should welcome such a guest as grief,
Save bidding farewell to so sweet a guest
As my sweet Richard. Yet again methinks
Some unborn sorrow, ripe in fortune's womb,
Is coming towards me, and my inward soul
With nothing trembles. At some thing it grieves
More than with parting from my lord the King.

I said that to please the King; I can't do it to please myself; however I don't know why I have become quite so depressed apart from the fact that I've had to say farewell to someone as sweet as my Richard. But I have a feeling that's there is a bad time brewing, coming towards me, and I am disturbed for no reason. Something is upsetting me more than just my parting from my lord the King.

BUSHY.
Each substance of a grief hath twenty shadows,
Which shows like grief itself, but is not so;
For sorrow's eye, glazed with blinding tears,
Divides one thing entire to many objects,
Like perspectives which, rightly gaz'd upon,
Show nothing but confusion-ey'd awry,
Distinguish form. So your sweet Majesty,
Looking awry upon your lord's departure,
Find shapes of grief more than himself to wail;
Which, look'd on as it is, is nought but shadows
Of what it is not. Then, thrice-gracious Queen,
More than your lord's departure weep not-more is not
seen;
Or if it be, 'tis with false sorrow's eye,
Which for things true weeps things imaginary.

Every real sorrow has twenty shadows, which look like sorrow but are not, the sorrowing eye, covered with blinding tears, splits one thing into many objects, like a perspective picture which, observed face on, shows nothing but confusion—looked at from an angle, you can see the shape. So your sweet Majesty, looking slantwise at your lord's departure, finds more things than that to worry about; if you look at it clearly those are nothing but shadows that don't exist. So, most gracious Queen, don't weep for more than your lord's departure—there is nothing more; or if there is, it's just created by your sorrow, which real sadness makes you weep for

QUEEN.
It may be so; but yet my inward soul
Persuades me it is otherwise. Howe'er it be,
I cannot but be sad; so heavy sad
As-though, on thinking, on no thought I think-
Makes me with heavy nothing faint and shrink.

BUSHY.
'Tis nothing but conceit, my gracious lady.

QUEEN.
'Tis nothing less: conceit is still deriv'd
From some forefather grief; mine is not so,
For nothing hath begot my something grief,
Or something hath the nothing that I grieve;
'Tis in reversion that I do possess-
But what it is that is not yet known what,
I cannot name; 'tis nameless woe, I wot.

Enter GREEN

GREEN.
God save your Majesty! and well met, gentlemen.
I hope the King is not yet shipp'd for Ireland.

QUEEN.
Why hopest thou so? 'Tis better hope he is;
For his designs crave haste, his haste good hope.
Then wherefore dost thou hope he is not shipp'd?

GREEN.
That he, our hope, might have retir'd his power
And driven into despair an enemy's hope
Who strongly hath set footing in this land.
The banish'd Bolingbroke repeals himself,
And with uplifted arms is safe arriv'd
At Ravenspurgh.

QUEEN.

imaginary things.

*You may be right, but deep down
I feel differently. Whatever the case,
I can't help being depressed; so deeply
depressed that even though I try not to
think I end up feeling crushed under the
weight of nothingness.*

*That's just your imagination, my gracious
lady.*

*It's anything but: imagination still springs
from some previous sorrow; this isn't the
case, for nothing created my current grief,
or someone else's suffering it at the
moment; I will get it when they have
finished with it– but what this unknown
thing could be, I can't say; I suppose you
would call it a nameless dread.*

*God save your Majesty! Good to see you,
gentlemen. I hope the King has not set sail
for Ireland yet.*

*Why do you hope that? You should be
hoping he has; his plans demand speed,
the quicker he is the better chance. So why
do you hope he's not sailed?*

*So that he, our hope, might have recalled
his forces and destroyed the hopes of
our enemies who have got a strong
foothold in this country. The exiled
Bolingbroke has forgiven himself, and has
arrived safely, looking for battle, at
Ravenspurgh.*

Now God in heaven forbid!

GREEN.
Ah, madam, 'tis too true; and that is worse,
The Lord Northumberland, his son young Henry Percy,
The Lords of Ross, Beaumond, and Willoughby,
With all their powerful friends, are fled to him.

BUSHY.
Why have you not proclaim'd Northumberland
And all the rest revolted faction traitors?

GREEN.
We have; whereupon the Earl of Worcester
Hath broken his staff, resign'd his stewardship,
And all the household servants fled with him
To Bolingbroke.

QUEEN.
So, Green, thou art the midwife to my woe,
And Bolingbroke my sorrow's dismal heir.
Now hath my soul brought forth her prodigy;
And I, a gasping new-deliver'd mother,
Have woe to woe, sorrow to sorrow join'd.

BUSHY.
Despair not, madam.

QUEEN.
Who shall hinder me?
I will despair, and be at enmity
With cozening hope-he is a flatterer,
A parasite, a keeper-back of death,
Who gently would dissolve the bands of life,
Which false hope lingers in extremity.

Enter YORK

GREEN.

God forbid that this is true!

Ah, madam, it's too true; and what's worse, Lord Northumberland, his son young Henry Percy, the Lords of Ross, Beaumon, and Willoughby, with all their powerful friends, have joined him.

Why have you not declared Northumberland and all the rest of the rebels as traitors?

We have; which made the Earl of Worcester break his staff, resign his stewardship, and he has fled with all the household servants to Bolingbroke.

So, Green, you are the midwife of my sorrow, and Bolingbroke is the miserable birth of it. Now my suspicions have been confirmed, and, gasping like a mother who's just given birth, I suffer woe on woe, sorrow on sorrow.

Do not despair, madam.

Who's going to stop me? I will despair, and fight against cheating hope-he is a flatterer, a parasite, he postpones death, which can gently remove the burden of life, while false hope makes us suffer it to the end.

Here comes the Duke of York.

QUEEN.
With signs of war about his aged neck.
O, full of careful business are his looks!
Uncle, for God's sake, speak comfortable words.

YORK.
Should I do so, I should belie my thoughts.
Comfort's in heaven; and we are on the earth,
Where nothing lives but crosses, cares, and grief.
Your husband, he is gone to save far off,
Whilst others come to make him lose at home.
Here am I left to underprop his land,
Who, weak with age, cannot support myself.
Now comes the sick hour that his surfeit made;
Now shall he try his friends that flatter'd him.

Enter a SERVINGMAN

SERVINGMAN.
My lord, your son was gone before I came.

YORK.
He was-why so go all which way it will!
The nobles they are fled, the commons they are cold
And will, I fear, revolt on Hereford's side.
Sirrah, get thee to Plashy, to my sister Gloucester;
Bid her send me presently a thousand pound.
Hold, take my ring.

SERVINGMAN.
My lord, I had forgot to tell your lordship,
To-day, as I came by, I called there-
But I shall grieve you to report the rest.

YORK.
What is't, knave?

SERVINGMAN.
An hour before I came, the Duchess died.

Here comes the Duke of York.

With his arm around his old neck.
He looks anxious and preoccupied!
Uncle, for God's sake, say something
hopeful.

If I did, I would be being dishonest.
Hope is in heaven; and we are on earth,
where there is nothing but treachery, care
and sorrow. Your husband has gone to
save his far-off lands while others come
to take his lands at home. Here am I, left
to prop up his country, who, weak with
age, cannot even support myself. This is
the sickness brought on by his excesses;
now he'll see what those friends who
flattered him are like.

My lord, your son had gone before I came.

Had he-well then whatever happens,
happens! The nobles have fled, the
common people are unsympathetic and
will, I fear, fight for Hereford. Sir, go to
Plashy, to my sister Gloucester; tell her to
send me a thousand pounds at once.
Wait, take my ring.

My Lord, I had forgotten to tell your
lordship, today, as I passed by, I called in
there- but the rest will upset you.

What is it, scoundrel?

The Duchess had died an hour before I

arrived.

YORK.
God for his mercy! what a tide of woes
Comes rushing on this woeful land at once!
I know not what to do. I would to God,
So my untruth had not provok'd him to it,
The King had cut off my head with my brother's.
What, are there no posts dispatch'd for Ireland?
How shall we do for money for these wars?
Come, sister-cousin, I would say-pray, pardon me.
Go, fellow, get thee home, provide some carts,
And bring away the armour that is there.
 Exit SERVINGMAN
Gentlemen, will you go muster men?
If I know how or which way to order these affairs
Thus disorderly thrust into my hands,
Never believe me. Both are my kinsmen.
T'one is my sovereign, whom both my oath
And duty bids defend; t'other again
Is my kinsman, whom the King hath wrong'd,
Whom conscience and my kindred bids to right.
Well, somewhat we must do.-Come, cousin,
I'll dispose of you. Gentlemen, go muster up your men
And meet me presently at Berkeley.
I should to Plashy too,
But time will not permit. All is uneven,
And everything is left at six and seven.

May God have mercy, what a tide of sorrow comes rushing over this sad land at once! I don't know what to do, I wish to God, as long as it wasn't because of any disloyalty, that the King had cut my head off with my brother's. What, has nobody sent messages to Ireland? How shall we pay for these wars? Come, sister–cousin, I should say, please excuse me. Go, fellow, go home, get some carts and bring the armour which is there. Gentlemen, will you go and gather your forces? If I say I know how to deal with this business which has been thrust so chaotically into my hands, don't believe me. They are both my kinsmen: one is my king, who I am bound by oath and duty to defend; but then the other is my kinsman, whom the king has wronged, and my conscience and my kinship with him tells me to side with him. Well, we must do something. Come, cousin, I'll see you safe. Gentleman, go and gather your forces, and meet me at once at Berkeley. I should go to Plashy too, but there's't time. Everything is disordered, it's all at sixes and sevens.

Exeunt YORK and QUEEN

BUSHY.
The wind sits fair for news to go to Ireland.
But none returns. For us to levy power
Proportionable to the enemy
Is all unpossible.

It's a good wind to take news to Ireland, but none comes back. It's completely impossible for us to raise forces which could match the enemy.

GREEN.
Besides, our nearness to the King in love
Is near the hate of those love not the King.

Besides, our love for the King is pretty much equal to the hatred of those who do not love him.

BAGOT.
And that is the wavering commons; for their love

And those are the changeable common

Lies in their purses; and whoso empties them,
By so much fills their hearts with deadly hate.

BUSHY.
Wherein the King stands generally condemn'd.

BAGOT.
If judgment lie in them, then so do we,
Because we ever have been near the King.

GREEN.
Well, I will for refuge straight to Bristow Castle.
The Earl of Wiltshire is already there.

BUSHY.
Thither will I with you; for little office
Will the hateful commons perform for us,
Except like curs to tear us all to pieces.
Will you go along with us?

BAGOT.
No; I will to Ireland to his Majesty.
Farewell. If heart's presages be not vain,
We three here part that ne'er shall meet again.

BUSHY.
That's as York thrives to beat back Bolingbroke.

GREEN.
Alas, poor Duke! the task he undertakes
Is numb'ring sands and drinking oceans dry.
Where one on his side fights, thousands will fly.
Farewell at once-for once, for all, and ever.

BUSHY.
Well, we may meet again.

BAGOT.
I fear me, never.

---

*people; their love depends on their purses;
anyone who empties them puts the same
amount of hate in their hearts.*

*And so the king is widely condemned for
that.*

*If judgement depends on them, we are
condemned too, because of our closeness
to the King.*

*Well, I will seek refuge at once in Bristow
Castle. The Earl of Wiltshire is already
there.*

*I'll go there with you; we won't get
any favours from the common people,
they'll just tear us to pieces like dogs.
Will you come along with us?*

*No; I will go to the king in Ireland.
Farewell. If my suspicions are correct,
we three shall never meet again.*

*That depends on whether York manages to
defeat Bolingbroke.*

*Alas, poor Duke! He might as well try
to count the sand and drink the oceans
dry. For every one who fights on his side,
thousands will desert. Farewell at
once–for once, for all, and for ever.*

Well, we may meet again.

I fear we never will.

Exeunt

SCENE III.

Gloucestershire

Enter BOLINGBROKE and NORTHUMBERLAND, forces

BOLINGBROKE.
How far is it, my lord, to Berkeley now?

How far is it, my lord, to Berkeley now?

NORTHUMBERLAND.
Believe me, noble lord,
I am a stranger here in Gloucestershire.
These high wild hills and rough uneven ways
Draws out our miles, and makes them wearisome;
And yet your fair discourse hath been as sugar,
Making the hard way sweet and delectable.
But I bethink me what a weary way
From Ravenspurgh to Cotswold will be found
In Ross and Willoughby, wanting your company,
Which, I protest, hath very much beguil'd
The tediousness and process of my travel.
But theirs is sweet'ned with the hope to have
The present benefit which I possess;
And hope to joy is little less in joy
Than hope enjoy'd. By this the weary lords
Shall make their way seem short, as mine hath done
By sight of what I have, your noble company.

Believe me, noble Lord,
I am a stranger here in Gloucestershire.
These wild high hills and rough uneven
roads make our journey seem longer and
more tiring, and yet your fair speech has
been like sugar, making this hard journey
sweet and delightful. But I think about
what a weary journey it will be from
Ravenspurgh to the Cotswolds for Ross
and Willoughby, without your company,
which I must say has very much
compensated for the tedious process of my
travels. But their journey is sweetened
with the hope of gaining   the benefits
which I now have, and to hope for
happiness is almost as good as having it.
This will make the journey seem shorter
for the weary lords, as your noble
company has done for me.

BOLINGBROKE.
Of much less value is my company
Than your good words. But who comes here?

Your kind words are worth much more
than my company. But who is this?

Enter HARRY PERCY

NORTHUMBERLAND.
It is my son, young Harry Percy,
Sent from my brother Worcester, whencesoever.
Harry, how fares your uncle?

It is my son, young Harry Percy,
sent from my brother Worcester, wherever
he is. Harry, how is your uncle getting on?

PERCY.

I had thought, my lord, to have learn'd his health of you.

I thought, my lord, that I would have learned that from you.

NORTHUMBERLAND.
Why, is he not with the Queen?

Why, is he not with the Queen?

PERCY.
No, my good lord; he hath forsook the court,
Broken his staff of office, and dispers'd
The household of the King.

No, my good lord; he has left the court, broken his staff of office, and sent away all the King's servants.

NORTHUMBERLAND.
What was his reason?
He was not so resolv'd when last we spake together.

Why did he do this? He wasn't that way inclined last time we spoke.

PERCY.
Because your lordship was proclaimed traitor.
But he, my lord, is gone to Ravenspurgh,
To offer service to the Duke of Hereford;
And sent me over by Berkeley, to discover
What power the Duke of York had levied there;
Then with directions to repair to Ravenspurgh.

Because your lordship has been declared a traitor. But he, my lord, has gone to Ravenspurgh, to offer his services to the Duke of Hereford; he sent me over via Berkeley, to discover what forces the Duke of York had raised there; then I have orders to go on to Ravenspurgh.

NORTHUMBERLAND.
Have you forgot the Duke of Hereford, boy?

Have you forgotten the Duke of Hereford, boy?

PERCY.
No, my good lord; for that is not forgot
Which ne'er I did remember; to my knowledge,
I never in my life did look on him.

No, my good lord; I can't forget something which I have never known; as far as I know, I have never seen him in my life.

NORTHUMBERLAND.
Then learn to know him now; this is the Duke.

Then get to know him now; this is the Duke.

PERCY.
My gracious lord, I tender you my service,
Such as it is, being tender, raw, and young;
Which elder days shall ripen, and confirm
To more approved service and desert.

My gracious lord, I offer you my service, such as it is, being tender, raw and young; it will get better with time, and be able to serve you better, with better reward.

BOLINGBROKE.

I thank thee, gentle Percy; and be sure
I count myself in nothing else so happy
As in a soul rememb'ring my good friends;
And as my fortune ripens with thy love,
It shall be still thy true love's recompense.
My heart this covenant makes, my hand thus seals it.

I thank you, kind Percy; and rest assured that nothing makes me happier than remembering my good friends in my heart; as my fortunes increase with your love, you shall be rewarded. I make this contract with my heart, and seal it with a handshake.

NORTHUMBERLAND.
How far is it to Berkeley? And what stir
Keeps good old York there with his men of war?

How far is it to Berkeley? And what event keeps good old York there with his forces?

PERCY.
There stands the castle, by yon tuft of trees,
Mann'd with three hundred men, as I have heard;
And in it are the Lords of York, Berkeley, and
Seymour-
None else of name and noble estimate.

There is the castle, by that stand of trees, guarded by three hundred men, my reports inside are the Lords of York, Berkeley and Seymour— nobody else of importance.

Enter Ross and WILLOUGHBY

NORTHUMBERLAND.
Here come the Lords of Ross and Willoughby,
Bloody with spurring, fiery-red with haste.

Here come the Lords of Ross and Willoughby, their horses are bloody with spurring, they are bright red with hurry.

BOLINGBROKE.
Welcome, my lords. I wot your love pursues
A banish'd traitor. All my treasury
Is yet but unfelt thanks, which, more enrich'd,
Shall be your love and labour's recompense.

Welcome, my lords. I know you're following, for love, a banished traitor. All I can offer you at the moment is intangible thanks, but when I get more, I will reward your love and your efforts.

ROSS.
Your presence makes us rich, most noble lord.

Your presence makes us rich, most noble lord.

WILLOUGHBY.
And far surmounts our labour to attain it.

And is worth far more than the work we had to gain it.

BOLINGBROKE.
Evermore thanks, the exchequer of the poor;
Which, till my infant fortune comes to years,

More thanks, the Treasury of the poor; until my potential fortune is realised

Stands for my bounty. But who comes here?

take my thanks as an IOU. But who is this?

Enter BERKELEY

NORTHUMBERLAND.
It is my Lord of Berkeley, as I guess.

I think it is my Lord of Berkeley.

BERKELEY.
My Lord of Hereford, my message is to you.

My Lord of Hereford, my message is to you.

BOLINGBROKE.
My lord, my answer is-'to Lancaster';
And I am come to seek that name in England;
And I must find that title in your tongue
Before I make reply to aught you say.

*My lord, my answer is– 'to Lancaster';
I have come to find that title in England;
and you must use it to me
before I reply to anything you say.*

BERKELEY.
Mistake me not, my lord; 'tis not my meaning
To raze one title of your honour out.
To you, my lord, I come-what lord you will-
From the most gracious regent of this land,
The Duke of York, to know what pricks you on
To take advantage of the absent time,
And fright our native peace with self-borne arms.

*Don't mistake me, my lord; I have no
intention of depriving you of any of your
honourable titles. I come to you, my
lord–whatever lord you want to be– from
the most gracious regent of this land, the
Duke of York, to ask why you are taking
advantage of the King's absence and
disturbing the peace of the country with
your forces.*

Enter YORK, attended

BOLINGBROKE.
I shall not need transport my words by you;
Here comes his Grace in person. My noble uncle!

*I don't need to pass on my message
through you; here comes his grace in
person. My noble uncle!*

[Kneels]

YORK.
Show me thy humble heart, and not thy knee,
Whose duty is deceivable and false.

*Show me your humble heart, don't just
kneel, anybody can fake that.*

BOLINGBROKE.
My gracious uncle!-

My gracious uncle!–

YORK.

Tut, tut!
Grace me no grace, nor uncle me no uncle.
I am no traitor's uncle; and that word 'grace'
In an ungracious mouth is but profane.
Why have those banish'd and forbidden legs
Dar'd once to touch a dust of England's ground?
But then more 'why?'-why have they dar'd to march
So many miles upon her peaceful bosom,
Frighting her pale-fac'd villages with war
And ostentation of despised arms?
Com'st thou because the anointed King is hence?
Why, foolish boy, the King is left behind,
And in my loyal bosom lies his power.
Were I but now lord of such hot youth
As when brave Gaunt, thy father, and myself
Rescued the Black Prince, that young Mars of men,
From forth the ranks of many thousand French,
O, then how quickly should this arm of mine,
Now prisoner to the palsy, chastise the
And minister correction to thy fault!

Tut tut!
Don't call me your grace, and don't call
me uncle. I am not a traitor's uncle; and
that the word "grace" in the mouth of the
ungracious is a blasphemy. Why have
those exiled and banned legs dared to set
foot on a grain of England's soil? More
importantly, why? Why have they dared
to march so many miles across her
peaceful lands, frightening her palefaced
villages with war and flourishing your
hated weapons? Have you come because
the God appointed king is not here? Why,
foolish boy, the King has been left behind,
his power lies within my loyal heart. If I
still possessed my passionate youth, as I
did when brave Gaunt, your father, and
myself, rescued the Black Prince, that
young earthly Mars, from out of the ranks
of so many thousand Frenchmen, how
quickly then this arm of mine, now
handicapped with shaking, would punish
you, and show you the error of your ways!

BOLINGBROKE.
My gracious uncle, let me know my fault;
On what condition stands it and wherein?

My gracious uncle, let me know what my
fault is; how has it shown itself?

YORK.
Even in condition of the worst degree
In gross rebellion and detested treason.
Thou art a banish'd man, and here art come
Before the expiration of thy time,
In braving arms against thy sovereign.

By committing the worst thing that can be
done— horrible rebellion and hated
treason. You are an exile, and you have
come here before your term was up,
bearing arms against your king.

BOLINGBROKE.
As I was banish'd, I was banish'd Hereford;
But as I come, I come for Lancaster.
And, noble uncle, I beseech your Grace
Look on my wrongs with an indifferent eye.
You are my father, for methinks in you
I see old Gaunt alive. O, then, my father,
Will you permit that I shall stand condemn'd
A wandering vagabond; my rights and royalties
Pluck'd from my arms perforce, and given away
To upstart unthrifts? Wherefore was I born?

I was exiled as Hereford; I have returned
as Lancaster. And, noble uncle, I beg your
Grace to consider my complaints
impartially. You are my father, for I think
that I can see old Gaunt alive in you. Oh
then my father, do you agree that I should
be condemned to be a wandering
vagabond, that my rights and property
should be torn out of my arms by force,
and given away to vulgar wastrels? Why

If that my cousin king be King in England,
It must be granted I am Duke of Lancaster.
You have a son, Aumerle, my noble cousin;
Had you first died, and he been thus trod down,
He should have found his uncle Gaunt a father
To rouse his wrongs and chase them to the bay.
I am denied to sue my livery here,
And yet my letters patents give me leave.
My father's goods are all distrain'd and sold;
And these and all are all amiss employ'd.
What would you have me do? I am a subject,
And I challenge law-attorneys are denied me;
And therefore personally I lay my claim
To my inheritance of free descent.

was I born? If my cousin the king is king of England, it must be granted that I am the Duke of Lancaster. You have a son, Aumerle, my noble cousin; if you had died first, and he had been crushed like this, his uncle Gaunt would have been a father to him, discovering his wrongs and hunting them down. I have been forbidden the rights to my title, but my official documents prove I should have them. My father's property has all been confiscated and sold, and all the profits from that are being misused. What do you think I should do? I am a subject, and I am challenging the law; I am not allowed an attorney, and so I am putting my claim for my rightful inheritance in person.

NORTHUMBERLAND.
The noble Duke hath been too much abused.

The noble duke has suffered too much injustice.

ROSS.
It stands your Grace upon to do him right.

Your Grace is obliged to do right by him.

WILLOUGHBY.
Base men by his endowments are made great.

Low men have been given his inheritance.

YORK.
My lords of England, let me tell you this:
I have had feeling of my cousin's wrongs,
And labour'd all I could to do him right;
But in this kind to come, in braving arms,
Be his own carver and cut out his way,
To find out right with wrong-it may not be;
And you that do abet him in this kind
Cherish rebellion, and are rebels all.

My Lords of England, let me tell you this: I have appreciated the wrongs my cousin has suffered, and done all I could to put them right; but to come like this, carrying weapons, to be his own carver and cut out his path, to set things right by doing wrong—that cannot be; and anybody who helps him with this loves rebellion, and is a rebel.

NORTHUMBERLAND.
The noble Duke hath sworn his coming is
But for his own; and for the right of that
We all have strongly sworn to give him aid;
And let him never see joy that breaks that oath!

The noble duke has sworn he's only here to get what is his; and we have solemnly sworn to help him regain his rights; and may anyone who breaks that oath never be forgiven!

YORK.
Well, well, I see the issue of these arms.
I cannot mend it, I must needs confess,
Because my power is weak and all ill left;
But if I could, by Him that gave me life,
I would attach you all and make you stoop
Unto the sovereign mercy of the King;
But since I cannot, be it known unto you
I do remain as neuter. So, fare you well;
Unless you please to enter in the castle,
And there repose you for this night.

BOLINGBROKE.
An offer, uncle, that we will accept.
But we must win your Grace to go with us
To Bristow Castle, which they say is held
By Bushy, Bagot, and their complices,
The caterpillars of the commonwealth,
Which I have sworn to weed and pluck away.

YORK.
It may be I will go with you; but yet I'll pause,
For I am loath to break our country's laws.
Nor friends nor foes, to me welcome you are.
Things past redress are now with me past care.

Exeunt

Well, well, I can see where this war will end. I cannot stop it, I must admit, because my forces are weak and inadequate; but if I could, I swear by God, I would arrest you all and make you bow to the royal mercy of the King; but since I cannot, I shall tell you that I will remain neutral. So, farewell; unless you wish to come into the castle, and stay there for tonight.

We will accept that offer, uncle. But we must persuade your Grace to come with us to Bristow Castle, which they say is held by Bushy, Bagot and their accomplices, the parasites of this society, whom I have sworn to weed out and throw away.

I might possibly go with you; but I will think about it, because I'm very reluctant to break the laws of our country. You are neither friends nor foes, but you are welcome. I no longer care about things which I can't change.

SCENE IV.

A camp in Wales

Enter EARL OF SALISBURY and a WELSH CAPTAIN

CAPTAIN.
My Lord of Salisbury, we have stay'd ten days
And hardly kept our countrymen together,
And yet we hear no tidings from the King;
Therefore we will disperse ourselves. Farewell.

My Lord of Salisbury, we have waited ten days, and valiantly kept our countrymen together, and yet we have heard no news from the King; therefore we shall leave. Farewell.

SALISBURY.
Stay yet another day, thou trusty Welshman;
The King reposeth all his confidence in thee.

Stay just another day, you trusty Welshman; the King puts all his trust in you.

CAPTAIN.
'Tis thought the King is dead; we will not stay.
The bay trees in our country are all wither'd,
And meteors fright the fixed stars of heaven;
The pale-fac'd moon looks bloody on the earth,
And lean-look'd prophets whisper fearful change;
Rich men look sad, and ruffians dance and leap-
The one in fear to lose what they enjoy,
The other to enjoy by rage and war.
These signs forerun the death or fall of kings.
Farewell. Our countrymen are gone and fled,
As well assur'd Richard their King is dead.

It's thought the King is dead; we won't stay. The bay trees in our country are all shrivelled, and meteors terrify the fixed stars of heaven; the pale faced moon looks bloodily on the earth, and haggard looking prophets whisper of terrible changes; rich men look sad, and scoundrels dance and leap– one in fear of losing what they have, the other to have those things through riot and war. These signs are omens of the death of all of kings. Farewell. My countrymen have gone and fled, certain that Richard their king is dead.

Exit

SALISBURY.
Ah, Richard, with the eyes of heavy mind,
I see thy glory like a shooting star
Fall to the base earth from the firmament!
The sun sets weeping in the lowly west,
Witnessing storms to come, woe, and unrest;

Ah, Richard, with the eyes of sorrow, I can see your glory like a shooting star falling from the heavens onto the low earth! The sun is setting weeping in the West, showing the storms to come, sorrow

Thy friends are fled, to wait upon thy foes;
And crossly to thy good all fortune goes.

and unrest; your friends have fled to serve your enemies; and everything is going against you.

Exit

ACT III.

SCENE I.

BOLINGBROKE'S camp at Bristol

Enter BOLINGBROKE, YORK, NORTHUMBERLAND, PERCY, ROSS, WILLOUGHBY, BUSHY and GREEN, prisoners

BOLINGBROKE.
Bring forth these men.
Bushy and Green, I will not vex your souls-
Since presently your souls must part your bodies-
With too much urging your pernicious lives,
For 'twere no charity; yet, to wash your blood
From off my hands, here in the view of men
I will unfold some causes of your deaths:
You have misled a prince, a royal king,
A happy gentleman in blood and lineaments,
By you unhappied and disfigured clean;
You have in manner with your sinful hours
Made a divorce betwixt his queen and him;
Broke the possession of a royal bed,
And stain'd the beauty of a fair queen's cheeks
With tears drawn from her eyes by your foul wrongs;
Myself-a prince by fortune of my birth,
Near to the King in blood, and near in love
Till you did make him misinterpret me-
Have stoop'd my neck under your injuries
And sigh'd my English breath in foreign clouds,
Eating the bitter bread of banishment,
Whilst you have fed upon my signories,
Dispark'd my parks and fell'd my forest woods,
From my own windows torn my household coat,
Raz'd out my imprese, leaving me no sign
Save men's opinions and my living blood
To show the world I am a gentleman.
This and much more, much more than twice all this,
Condemns you to the death. See them delivered over
To execution and the hand of death.

Bring out these men.
Bushy and Greene, I will not torment your souls, since soon they will be leaving your bodies, by dwelling too much on your evil lives, that would be uncharitable; but, to wash your blood from my hands, I will reveal in public some of the reasons why you must die: you led a Prince, a Royal King, astray, the gentleman who was fortunate in his birth and body, you made him unhappy and soiled him; your sinful behaviour has created a sort of divorce between his queen and him, broken the covenant of the royal marriage, and stained the beauty of a fair queen's cheeks with tears, caused by your foul behaviour; I myself–a prince by birth, a close relation of the King, and loved by him, until you persuaded him to misunderstand me– have suffered from the wrongs you have done, and breathed my English breath in foreign climates, eating the bitter bread of exile, while you grew fat on my estates, vandalised my parks and cut down my forests, smashed my windows with my coat of arms on them, defaced my motto, leaving no sign, apart from men's opinions and my physical presence, to show the world that I am a gentleman. This and much more, much more than double this, condemns you to death. Take them away to be executed and given to death.

BUSHY.
More welcome is the stroke of death to me
Than Bolingbroke to England. Lords, farewell.

*My execution is more welcome to me
Than Bolingbroke is to England. Lords,
farewell.*

GREEN.
My comfort is that heaven will take our souls,
And plague injustice with the pains of hell.

*I am comforted to think that heaven will
take us in, and torment those who do this
injustice with the pains of hell.*

BOLINGBROKE.

My Lord Northumberland, see them dispatch'd.

*Exeunt NORTHUMBERLAND, and
others, with the prisoners
My Lord Northumberland, see to their
execution.*

Uncle, you say the Queen is at your house;
For God's sake, fairly let her be entreated.
Tell her I send to her my kind commends;
Take special care my greetings be delivered.

*Uncle, you say the Queen is at your house;
for God's sake make sure she is fairly
treated. Tell her I send her my kind
greetings; take special care that this
message is delivered.*

YORK.
A gentleman of mine I have dispatch'd
With letters of your love to her at large.

*I have sent a gentleman of mine
with letters which fully explain your love
for her.*

BOLINGBROKE.
Thanks, gentle uncle. Come, lords, away,
To fight with Glendower and his complices.
Awhile to work, and after holiday.

*Thanks, kind uncle. Come, lords, let's go,
to fight with Glendower and his
accomplices. And we must work for a
while, and then we shall rest.*

Exeunt

SCENE II.

The coast of Wales. A castle in view

Drums. Flourish and colours. Enter the KING, the BISHOP OF
CARLISLE,
AUMERLE, and soldiers

KING RICHARD.
Barkloughly Castle call they this at hand?

*Do they call this place Barkloughly
Castle?*

AUMERLE.
Yea, my lord. How brooks your Grace the air
After your late tossing on the breaking seas?

*Yes, my lord. How does your Grace like
the air after your recent choppy journey
on the sea?*

KING RICHARD.
Needs must I like it well. I weep for joy
To stand upon my kingdom once again.
Dear earth, I do salute thee with my hand,
Though rebels wound thee with their horses' hoofs.
As a long-parted mother with her child
Plays fondly with her tears and smiles in meeting,
So weeping-smiling greet I thee, my earth,
And do thee favours with my royal hands.
Feed not thy sovereign's foe, my gentle earth,
Nor with thy sweets comfort his ravenous sense;
But let thy spiders, that suck up thy venom,
And heavy-gaited toads, lie in their way,
Doing annoyance to the treacherous feet
Which with usurping steps do trample thee;
Yield stinging nettles to mine enemies;
And when they from thy bosom pluck a flower,
Guard it, I pray thee, with a lurking adder,
Whose double tongue may with a mortal touch
Throw death upon thy sovereign's enemies.
Mock not my senseless conjuration, lords.
This earth shall have a feeling, and these stones
Prove armed soldiers, ere her native king
Shall falter under foul rebellion's arms.

*Naturally I like it: I weep for joy
to stand again in my kingdom.
Dear earth, I salute you with my hand,
although rebels are insulting you with the
hooves of their horses. Like a mother who
has been separated from her child for a
long time plays fondly with it with smiles
and tears when she meets, so weeping,
smiling, I greet you, my earth, and lay my
royal hands upon you; do not feed the
enemy of your king, my gentle earth, nor
give them any of your bounty to feed them,
but let your spiders that suck up your
poison and heavy footed toads lie in their
way, damaging their treacherous feet,
which trample over you with rebellious
steps; give my enemies stinging nettles;
and when they pick a flower from your
earth, please let it be guarded with a
hidden adder, whose forked tongue could
with its fateful touch gift death to your
king's enemies. Don't laugh at my talking
to senseless things, lords: this earth will
be capable of feeling, and the stones will*

turn into armed soldiers before her native king will fall under the assault of foul rebellion.

CARLISLE.
Fear not, my lord; that Power that made you king
Hath power to keep you king in spite of all.
The means that heaven yields must be embrac'd
And not neglected; else, if heaven would,
And we will not, heaven's offer we refuse,
The proffered means of succour and redress.

Don't worry, my lord; the power that made you King has the power to keep you king in spite of everything. We must embrace the opportunities heaven gives us, not neglect them; otherwise, if heaven desires something we don't do, we are refusing the offer of heaven, refusing the means of help and revenge.

AUMERLE.
He means, my lord, that we are too remiss;
Whilst Bolingbroke, through our security,
Grows strong and great in substance and in power.

He means, my lord, that we are not doing enough; meanwhile Bolingbroke, through our overconfidence, is growing great and strong in wealth and power.

KING RICHARD.
Discomfortable cousin! know'st thou not
That when the searching eye of heaven is hid,
Behind the globe, that lights the lower world,
Then thieves and robbers range abroad unseen
In murders and in outrage boldly here;
But when from under this terrestrial ball
He fires the proud tops of the eastern pines
And darts his light through every guilty hole,
Then murders, treasons, and detested sins,
The cloak of night being pluck'd from off their backs,
Stand bare and naked, trembling at themselves?
So when this thief, this traitor, Bolingbroke,
Who all this while hath revell'd in the night,
Whilst we were wand'ring with the Antipodes,
Shall see us rising in our throne, the east,
His treasons will sit blushing in his face,
Not able to endure the sight of day,
But self-affrighted tremble at his sin.
Not all the water in the rough rude sea
Can wash the balm off from an anointed king;
The breath of worldly men cannot depose
The deputy elected by the Lord.
For every man that Bolingbroke hath press'd
To lift shrewd steel against our golden crown,
God for his Richard hath in heavenly pay

Discouraging cousin! Don't you know that when the sun dips below the horizon and lights the bottom of the world, then the thieves and robbers roam about unseen here, boldly committing murders and outrages; but when the sun comes out from under the earth he lights up the proud tops of the eastern pines, and shines his light into every guilty hiding place, then murder, treason and revolting sins, having had the cloak of night plucked off their backs, stand there naked, trembling at themselves? So when this thief, this traitor, Bolingbroke, who has enjoyed himself all through the night, while we were wandering down below, will see us rising on our throne in the East, his treason will light up his face, he won't be able to tolerate the sight of day, but frightened by himself he will tremble at his sin. All the water in the rough rude sea cannot wash off the anointing oil of a king; the words of mortal men cannot overthrow the deputy chosen by the Lord; for every man that Bolingbroke has

A glorious angel. Then, if angels fight,
Weak men must fall; for heaven still guards the right.

conscripted to raise a harmful sword against my golden crown, God has a glorious angel as a heavenly servant for his Richard: so, if angels fight, weak men must fall, for heaven still defends the just.

Enter SALISBURY

Welcome, my lord. How far off lies your power?

Welcome, my lord: how far away are your forces?

SALISBURY.
Nor near nor farther off, my gracious lord,
Than this weak arm. Discomfort guides my tongue,
And bids me speak of nothing but despair.
One day too late, I fear me, noble lord,
Hath clouded all thy happy days on earth.
O, call back yesterday, bid time return,
And thou shalt have twelve thousand fighting men!
To-day, to-day, unhappy day, too late,
O'erthrows thy joys, friends, fortune, and thy state;
For all the Welshmen, hearing thou wert dead,
Are gone to Bolingbroke, dispers'd, and fled.

As close to you, my gracious lord, as this weak arm is. Unhappiness guides my speech, and makes me speak of nothing but despair. I'm afraid, noble lord, you have come one day too late, and that has lost you your chance of happiness on earth. Oh, if it was only yesterday, if we could turn back time, you would have twelve thousand fighting men! Today, today, unhappy day, it's too late, your happiness, friends, fortune and your country are all lost; all the Welshmen, hearing you were dead have gone over to Bolingbroke, dispersed and fled.

AUMERLE.
Comfort, my liege, why looks your Grace so pale?

Be easy, my lord, why does your Grace look so pale?

KING RICHARD.
But now the blood of twenty thousand men
Did triumph in my face, and they are fled;
And, till so much blood thither come again,
Have I not reason to look pale and dead?
All souls that will be safe, fly from my side;
For time hath set a blot upon my pride.

Previously I had the blood of twenty thousand men lighting up my face, and they have fled; and, until I get that much blood back again, why shouldn't I look pale and dead? Anyone who wants to be safe, run away;
Time has ruined my position.

AUMERLE.
Comfort, my liege; remember who you are.

Be easy, my lord; remember who you are.

KING RICHARD.
I had forgot myself; am I not King?

I was forgetting myself; aren't I the King?

Awake, thou coward majesty! thou sleepest.
Is not the King's name twenty thousand names?
Arm, arm, my name! a puny subject strikes
At thy great glory. Look not to the ground,
Ye favourites of a king; are we not high?
High be our thoughts. I know my uncle York
Hath power enough to serve our turn. But who comes
 here?

Wake up, you cowardly royal! You're asleep. Isn't the King's name worth twenty thousand men? Take up your arms, my name! A puny subject is striking at your great glory. Don't be downcast, you King's favourites; aren't we noble? Let our thoughts be noble. I know my uncle York has enough forces for us. But who is this coming?

Enter SCROOP

SCROOP.
More health and happiness betide my liege
Than can my care-tun'd tongue deliver him.

May my lord have more health and happiness than my worried tongue can offer him.

KING RICHARD.
Mine ear is open and my heart prepar'd.
The worst is worldly loss thou canst unfold.
Say, is my kingdom lost? Why, 'twas my care,
And what loss is it to be rid of care?
Strives Bolingbroke to be as great as we?
Greater he shall not be; if he serve God,
We'll serve him too, and be his fellow so.
Revolt our subjects? That we cannot mend;
They break their faith to God as well as us.
Cry woe, destruction, ruin, and decay-
The worst is death, and death will have his day.

My ears are open and my heart is ready. The worst you can tell me is that I have lost worldly things. Tell me, is my kingdom lost? Why, it was my burden, what loss is it to lose a burden? Is Bolingbroke trying to be as great as me? He shall not be greater; if he serves God, I'll serve him too, and be his equal. Are our subjects rebelling? We can't change that; they are breaking their promise to God as well as to me. Tell me of sorrow, destruction, ruin and decay– the worst you can say is death, and he will always come.

SCROOP.
Glad am I that your Highness is so arm'd
To bear the tidings of calamity.
Like an unseasonable stormy day
Which makes the silver rivers drown their shores,
As if the world were all dissolv'd to tears,
So high above his limits swells the rage
Of Bolingbroke, covering your fearful land
With hard bright steel and hearts harder than steel.
White-beards have arm'd their thin and hairless scalps
Against thy majesty; boys, with women's voices,
Strive to speak big, and clap their female joints
In stiff unwieldy arms against thy crown;
Thy very beadsmen learn to bend their bows

*I'm glad that your Highness is so prepared to receive bad news.
Like a stormy day in summer which makes the silver rivers burst their banks, as if the whole world had dissolved into tears, that's as high as the rage of Bolingbroke has risen, flooding your fearful country with hard bright steel and hearts harder than steel. Old men have covered their bald heads with helmets to fight your Majesty; boys, with unbroken voices, try to speak like men, and slap their girlish hands in awkward assaults on*

Of double-fatal yew against thy state;
Yea, distaff-women manage rusty bills
Against thy seat: both young and old rebel,
And all goes worse than I have power to tell.

your crown; your own archers are bending their bows of deathdealing yew against your majesty; even servant women are wielding rusty pikes against your throne: both the young and the old rebel, and everything is going worse than I have power to describe.

KING RICHARD.
Too well, too well thou tell'st a tale so in.
Where is the Earl of Wiltshire? Where is Bagot?
What is become of Bushy? Where is Green?
That they have let the dangerous enemy
Measure our confines with such peaceful steps?
If we prevail, their heads shall pay for it.
I warrant they have made peace with Bolingbroke.

You have told your tale too well. Where is the Earl of Wiltshire? Where is Bagot? What has happened to Bushy? Where is Green? Why have they allowed the dangerous enemy to walk into our kingdom unopposed? If I win I shall have them executed for it. I'll bet they have made peace with Bolingbroke.

SCROOP.
Peace have they made with him indeed, my lord.

They have certainly made peace with him, my lord.

KING RICHARD.
O villains, vipers, damn'd without redemption!
Dogs, easily won to fawn on any man!
Snakes, in my heart-blood warm'd, that sting my heart!
Three Judases, each one thrice worse than Judas!
Would they make peace? Terrible hell make war
Upon their spotted souls for this offence!

Oh villains, vipers, damn them eternally! Dogs, who can be won over by any man! Snakes, warmed by my own blood, that sting my heart! Three Judases, each one three times worse than Judas! Make peace, would they? May terrible hell make war on their stained souls for this crime!

SCROOP.
Sweet love, I see, changing his property,
Turns to the sourest and most deadly hate.
Again uncurse their souls; their peace is made
With heads, and not with hands; those whom you curse
Have felt the worst of death's destroying wound
And lie full low, grav'd in the hollow ground.

I see that sweet love when changing his point of view can turn to the sourest and most deadly hate. Take your curse off their souls; they have made their peace with their heads, and not with their hands; those whom you curse have felt the heaviest wound of death and are lying low in their graves.

AUMERLE.
Is Bushy, Green, and the Earl of Wiltshire dead?

Are Bushy, Green, and the Earl of Wiltshire all dead?

SCROOP.

67

Ay, all of them at Bristow lost their heads.

AUMERLE.
Where is the Duke my father with his power?

KING RICHARD.
No matter where-of comfort no man speak.
Let's talk of graves, of worms, and epitaphs;
Make dust our paper, and with rainy eyes
Write sorrow on the bosom of the earth.
Let's choose executors and talk of wills;
And yet not so-for what can we bequeath
Save our deposed bodies to the ground?
Our lands, our lives, and an, are Bolingbroke's.
And nothing can we can our own but death
And that small model of the barren earth
Which serves as paste and cover to our bones.
For God's sake let us sit upon the ground
And tell sad stories of the death of kings:
How some have been depos'd, some slain in war,
Some haunted by the ghosts they have depos'd,
Some poison'd by their wives, some sleeping kill'd,
All murder'd-for within the hollow crown
That rounds the mortal temples of a king
Keeps Death his court; and there the antic sits,
Scoffing his state and grinning at his pomp;
Allowing him a breath, a little scene,
To monarchize, be fear'd, and kill with looks;
Infusing him with self and vain conceit,
As if this flesh which walls about our life
Were brass impregnable; and, humour'd thus,
Comes at the last, and with a little pin
Bores through his castle wall, and farewell, king!
Cover your heads, and mock not flesh and blood
With solemn reverence; throw away respect,
Tradition, form, and ceremonious duty;
For you have but mistook me all this while.
I live with bread like you, feel want,
Taste grief, need friends: subjected thus,
How can you say to me I am a king?

Yes, they were all executed at Bristol.

Where is my father the Duke with his forces?

It doesn't matter where, let nobody talk about hope. Let's talk about graves, worms and epitaphs, let's make the dust our paper, and without tears write of our sorrow on the face of the earth. Let's choose executors and talk of our wills. But let's not–for what can we leave apart from our overthrown bodies to the grave? Our lands, our lives and everything belong to Bolingbroke, and there is nothing we can call our own except for death; and that small mound of dead earth which seals in and covers our bones. For Godss sake let us sit upon the ground and tell sad stories of the death of Kings: how some have been deposed, some killed in war, some haunted by the ghosts they have overthrown, some poisoned by their wives, some killed when they were asleep, all murdered–for within the hollow crown which surrounds the mortal head of a king, that's where death lives, the grinning skull sits there, laughing at his royalty and grinning at his ceremony, allowing him a breath, a little scene, to be a king, to be feared and kill with a look; he fills him with selfishness and vanity, makes him think the flesh which contains our life is impregnable brass; and, once he's made him feel like this, death comes in the end, and drills through his castle wall with a little pin, and that's the end of the King! Cover your heads, and don't make fun of flesh and blood by worshipping it; throw away respect, tradition, formality and ceremonial duty; you have been mistaken about me all this time. I live on bread like you, I feel needs, I know sorrow, I need friends—when I'm like this, how can you say to me that I am a king?

CARLISLE.
My lord, wise men ne'er sit and wail their woes,
But presently prevent the ways to wail.
To fear the foe, since fear oppresseth strength,
Gives, in your weakness, strength unto your foe,
And so your follies fight against yourself.
Fear and be slain-no worse can come to fight;
And fight and die is death destroying death,
Where fearing dying pays death servile breath.

My lord, wise men never sit and bemoan their lot, but find ways to ease their sorrows. If you fear the enemy, since fear weakens your strength, your weakness gives strength to your enemy, and so your foolishness makes you fight against yourself. Be afraid and be killed—perhaps the worst you can get from fighting; to die fighting is to destroy death with death, whereas to be afraid of death means you pay him your whole life.

AUMERLE.
My father hath a power; inquire of him,
And learn to make a body of a limb.

My father has some forces; call him up, and learn to make a whole from a part.

KING RICHARD.
Thou chid'st me well. Proud Bolingbroke, I come
To change blows with thee for our day of doom.
This ague fit of fear is over-blown;
An easy task it is to win our own.
Say, Scroop, where lies our uncle with his power?
Speak sweetly, man, although thy looks be sour.

Your admonitions are correct. Proud Bolingbroke, I'm coming to exchange blows with you to decide our fate. This feverish fit of fear has blown over; it will be easy to win our rights. Tell me, Scroop, where is my uncle with his forces? Speaks sweetly, man, although you look sour.

SCROOP.
Men judge by the complexion of the sky
The state in inclination of the day;
So may you by my dull and heavy eye,
My tongue hath but a heavier tale to say.
I play the torturer, by small and small
To lengthen out the worst that must be spoken:
Your uncle York is join'd with Bolingbroke;
And all your northern castles yielded up,
And all your southern gentlemen in arms
Upon his party.

Men judge what time of day it is by the colour of the sky; so you can judge by my sorrowful eye that I still have worse things to say. I am a torturer, bit by bit I parcel out the worst things that can be said: your uncle York has joined forces with Bolingbroke; all your northern castles have surrendered, and all your knights of the south have joined with him.

KING RICHARD.
Thou hast said enough.
[To AUMERLE] Beshrew thee, cousin, which didst
 lead me forth

*You have said enough.
[To Aumerle] Damn you, cousin, who led me astray*

Of that sweet way I was in to despair!
What say you now? What comfort have we now?
By heaven, I'll hate him everlastingly
That bids me be of comfort any more.
Go to Flint Castle; there I'll pine away;
A king, woe's slave, shall kingly woe obey.
That power I have, discharge; and let them go
To ear the land that hath some hope to grow,
For I have none. Let no man speak again
To alter this, for counsel is but vain.

from that sweet path of despair I was following! Now what do you say? What hope do we have now? By heaven, I will forever hate anyone who ever tells me again to have hope. Let's go to Flint Castle; there I shall pine away; a King, the servant of sorrow, shall give in to his kingly sorrow. Let the forces that I have go free; let them go and plough the earth, if they have hopes that they can prosper, I have none. Let no man speak against me on this, their advice would be in vain.

AUMERLE.
My liege, one word.

dsMy lord, let me have just one word.

KING RICHARD.
He does me double wrong
That wounds me with the flatteries of his tongue.
Discharge my followers; let them hence away,
From Richard's night to Bolingbroke's fair day.

Anyone who wounds me with his flattery is doubly wronging me. Discharge my forces; let them go from here, from Richard's night to the fair day of Bolingbroke.

Exeunt

SCENE III.

Wales. Before Flint Castle

Enter, with drum and colours, BOLINGBROKE, YORK, NORTHUMBERLAND,
and forces

BOLINGBROKE.
So that by this intelligence we learn
The Welshmen are dispers'd; and Salisbury
Is gone to meet the King, who lately landed
With some few private friends upon this coast.

*So from this information we learn
that the Welshmenhave disbanded; and
Salisbury has gone to meet the King, who
recently landed on this coast with a few
private friends.*

NORTHUMBERLAND.
The news is very fair and good, my lord.
Richard not far from hence hath hid his head.

*The news is very good and favourable, my
lord. Richard has gone into hiding not far
from here.*

YORK.
It would beseem the Lord Northumberland
To say 'King Richard.' Alack the heavy day
When such a sacred king should hide his head!

*It would be more suitable for the Lord
Northumberland to say 'King Richard'.
What a sad day when such a sacred king
has to hide himself away!*

NORTHUMBERLAND.
Your Grace mistakes; only to be brief,
Left I his title out.

*Your Grace misunderstands me; I only
omitted his title for the sake of brevity.*

YORK.
The time hath been,
Would you have been so brief with him, he would
Have been so brief with you to shorten you,
For taking so the head, your whole head's length.

*There was a time
when if you had referred to him so briefly,
he would have shortened you as well,
for taking the head off his title, he would
have taken your head.*

BOLINGBROKE.
Mistake not, uncle, further than you should.

*Don't take more offence, uncle, than you
should.*

YORK.
Take not, good cousin, further than you should,

Don't take more liberties, good cousin,

71

Lest you mistake. The heavens are over our heads.

than you should, in case you make a mistake. God is watching us.

BOLINGBROKE.
I know it, uncle; and oppose not myself
Against their will. But who comes here?

I know it, uncle; and I don't want to go against His will. But who is this?

Enter PERCY

Welcome, Harry. What, will not this castle yield?

Welcome, Harry. What, won't this castle surrender?

PIERCY.
The castle royally is mann'd, my lord,
Against thy entrance.

The castle is royally guarded, my lord, against your entrance.

BOLINGBROKE.
Royally!
Why, it contains no king?

*Royally!
Why, is there a king in there?*

PERCY.
Yes, my good lord,
It doth contain a king; King Richard lies
Within the limits of yon lime and stone;
And with him are the Lord Aumerle, Lord Salisbury,
Sir Stephen Scroop, besides a clergyman
Of holy reverence; who, I cannot learn.

*Yes, my good lord,
it does contain a king; King Richard is within those walls of lime and stone; and with him on the Lord Aumerle, Lord Salisbury, Sir Stephen Scroop, as well as a clergyman of high position; I can't find out who he is.*

NORTHUMBERLAND.
O, belike it is the Bishop of Carlisle.

Oh, I should imagine it is the Bishop of Carlisle.

BOLINGBROKE.
[To NORTHUMBERLAND] Noble lord,
Go to the rude ribs of that ancient castle;
Through brazen trumpet send the breath of parley
Into his ruin'd ears, and thus deliver:
Henry Bolingbroke
On both his knees doth kiss King Richard's hand,
And sends allegiance and true faith of heart
To his most royal person; hither come
Even at his feet to lay my arms and power,
Provided that my banishment repeal'd
And lands restor'd again be freely granted;
If not, I'll use the advantage of my power
And lay the summer's dust with showers of blood

*Noble lord,
go to the rough walls of that ancient castle, and through its ruined loopholes blow a trumpet to announce your message, and tell them this: Henry Bolingbroke goes down on his knees and kisses King Richard's hand, and sends assurances of his loyalty and faithfulness to his royal person; I have come to lay my arms and my forces at his feet, provided that my banishment is repealed and that he freely grants the restoration of my lands; if he doesn't, I'll use my superior forces to lay*

Rain'd from the wounds of slaughtered Englishmen;
The which how far off from the mind of Bolingbroke
It is such crimson tempest should bedrench
The fresh green lap of fair King Richard's land,
My stooping duty tenderly shall show.
Go, signify as much, while here we march
Upon the grassy carpet of this plain.
[NORTHUMBERLAND advances to the Castle, with a trumpet]
Let's march without the noise of threat'ning drum,
That from this castle's tottered battlements
Our fair appointments may be well perus'd.
Methinks King Richard and myself should meet
With no less terror than the elements
Of fire and water, when their thund'ring shock
At meeting tears the cloudy cheeks of heaven.
Be he the fire, I'll be the yielding water;
The rage be his, whilst on the earth I rain
My waters-on the earth, and not on him.
March on, and mark King Richard how he looks.

the summer's dust with showers of blood raining from the wounds of slaughtered Englishmen– my kneeling to him like this shows just how unwilling Bolingbroke is that such a crimson storm should soak the fresh green ground of fair King Richard's land. Go, tell him as much, while we exercise here upon the grass of this plain. Let us march without any drums threatening an advance, so that from the tottering battlements of this castle they will get a good view of our forces' strength. I think King Richard and myself should meet with no less fear than the elements of fire and water, when they bring tears to the cloudy cheeks of heaven with the thundering shock of their meeting. He can be the fire, I'll be the surrendering water; he can be angry, while I rain my waters upon the earth–on the earth, and not on him. March on, and take note of how King Richard looks.

Parle without, and answer within; then a flourish.
Enter on the walls, the KING, the BISHOP OF CARLISLE,
AUMERLE, SCROOP, and SALISBURY

See, see, King Richard doth himself appear,
As doth the blushing discontented sun
From out the fiery portal of the east,
When he perceives the envious clouds are bent
To dim his glory and to stain the track
Of his bright passage to the occident.

See, see, King Richard himself appears, like the red sun when it rises unhappily from the fiery pillars of the East, when it sees that the jealous clouds are determined to dim his glory and to cover over his bright journey to the West.

YORK.
Yet he looks like a king. Behold, his eye,
As bright as is the eagle's, lightens forth
Controlling majesty. Alack, alack, for woe,
That any harm should stain so fair a show!

And yet he looks like a king. Look, his eye, as bright as an eagle's, flashes out his controlling majesty. Alas, alas, how sorrowful, if any harm comes to such a fair picture!

KING RICHARD.
[To NORTHUMBERLAND] We are amaz'd; and thus long
have we stood
To watch the fearful bending of thy knee,

I am astonished, I have stood here for some time

waiting to see you bend your knee in

Because we thought ourself thy lawful King;
And if we be, how dare thy joints forget
To pay their awful duty to our presence?
If we be not, show us the hand of God
That hath dismiss'd us from our stewardship;
For well we know no hand of blood and bone
Can gripe the sacred handle of our sceptre,
Unless he do profane, steal, or usurp.
And though you think that all, as you have done,
Have torn their souls by turning them from us,
And we are barren and bereft of friends,
Yet know-my master, God omnipotent,
Is mustering in his clouds on our behalf
Armies of pestilence; and they shall strike
Your children yet unborn and unbegot,
That lift your vassal hands against my head
And threat the glory of my precious crown.
Tell Bolingbroke, for yon methinks he stands,
That every stride he makes upon my land
Is dangerous treason; he is come to open
The purple testament of bleeding war;
But ere the crown he looks for live in peace,
Ten thousand bloody crowns of mothers' sons
Shall ill become the flower of England's face,
Change the complexion of her maid-pale peace
To scarlet indignation, and bedew
Her pastures' grass with faithful English blood.

NORTHUMBERLAND.
The King of Heaven forbid our lord the King
Should so with civil and uncivil arms
Be rush'd upon! Thy thrice noble cousin,
Harry Bolingbroke, doth humbly kiss thy hand;
And by the honourable tomb he swears
That stands upon your royal grandsire's bones,
And by the royalties of both your bloods,
Currents that spring from one most gracious head,
And by the buried hand of warlike Gaunt,
And by the worth and honour of himself,
Comprising all that may be sworn or said,
His coming hither hath no further scope
Than for his lineal royalties, and to beg
Enfranchisement immediate on his knees;

respect, because I thought I was your lawful king; and if I am, how dare your limbs forget to show their respects in my presence? If I am not, show me the hand of God that has dismissed me from my position; for I am certain that no mortal hand can grab the sacred handle of my sceptre, unless he is blaspheming, stealing or rebelling. And though you think that everyone has wounded their souls, as you have done, by turning away from me, and that I am powerless and friendless, you should know, my master, omnipotent God, is gathering plagues on my behalf in his clouds, and they will strike your as yet unborn children, unconceived, you who lift your servant's hands against my head, and threaten the glory of my precious crown. Tell Bolingbroke, for I think that's him over there, that every step he takes in my country is dangerous treason. He has come to open the purple book of bloody war. But before the crown he seeks can live in peace ten thousand bloody heads of mothers' sons shall stain the flowers of this English land, changing the complexion of her maidenly pale peace to scarlet anger, covering the grass of her fields with the blood of good Englishmen.

May God forbid that our lord the King should be attacked in such a rough way by his own citizens! Your trebly noble cousin, Harry Bolingbroke, humbly kisses your hand, and swears by the honourable tomb that stands over your royal grandfather's bones, and by the royal blood of both of you, which streams from the same glorious spring, and by the buried hand of warlike Gaunt, and by his own worth and honour, by anything that can be sworn or said, that he has only come here to claim his rightful inheritance, and to beg his immediate

Which on thy royal party granted once,
His glittering arms he will commend to rust,
His barbed steeds to stables, and his heart
To faithful service of your Majesty.
This swears he, as he is a prince, is just;
And as I am a gentleman I credit him.

reinstatement on his knees, and as soon as you, as King, agree to it, he will leave his glittering weapons to rust, send his warhorses back to the stables, and give his heart to the faithful service of your Majesty. He swears this as he is a prince and an honest man; and, as a gentleman, I believe him.

KING RICHARD.
Northumberland, say thus the King returns:
His noble cousin is right welcome hither;
And all the number of his fair demands
Shall be accomplish'd without contradiction.
With all the gracious utterance thou hast
Speak to his gentle hearing kind commends.
[To AUMERLE] We do debase ourselves, cousin, do
 we not,
To look so poorly and to speak so fair?
Shall we call back Northumberland, and send
Defiance to the traitor, and so die?

Northumberland, tell him this is the King's reply: his noble cousin is very welcome here; and every one of his reasonable demands

shall be fulfilled without argument. [To Aumerle] We are lowering ourselves, cousin, aren't we, to make such a poor show and to speak so fairly? Shall we call Northumberland back, and send defiant messages to the traitor, and so die?

AUMERLE.
No, good my lord; let's fight with gentle words
Till time lend friends, and friends their helpful swords.

No, my good lord; let's fight with gentle words until time gives us friends, and friends lend us the help of their swords.

KING RICHARD.
O God, O God! that e'er this tongue of mine
That laid the sentence of dread banishment
On yon proud man should take it off again
With words of sooth! O that I were as great
As is my grief, or lesser than my name!
Or that I could forget what I have been!
Or not remember what I must be now!
Swell'st thou, proud heart? I'll give thee scope to beat,
Since foes have scope to beat both thee and me.

Oh God, oh God! Why did this tongue of mine that imposed the dreaded sentence of exile on that proud man remove it with appeasing words! I wish I was as great as my grief, or smaller than my name! Or that I can forget what I have been! Or that I could forget what I now have to be! Are you swelling, proud heart? I'll give you an opportunity to beat, since your enemies have the opportunity to beat both you and me.

AUMERLE.
Northumberland comes back from Bolingbroke.

Northumberland is coming back from Bolingbroke.

KING RICHARD.

What must the King do now? Must he submit?
The King shall do it. Must he be depos'd?
The King shall be contented. Must he lose
The name of king? A God's name, let it go.
I'll give my jewels for a set of beads,
My gorgeous palace for a hermitage,
My gay apparel for an almsman's gown,
My figur'd goblets for a dish of wood,
My sceptre for a palmer's walking staff,
My subjects for a pair of carved saints,
And my large kingdom for a little grave,
A little little grave, an obscure grave-
Or I'll be buried in the king's high way,
Some way of common trade, where subjects' feet
May hourly trample on their sovereign's head;
For on my heart they tread now whilst I live,
And buried once, why not upon my head?
Aumerle, thou weep'st, my tender-hearted cousin!
We'll make foul weather with despised tears;
Our sighs and they shall lodge the summer corn
And make a dearth in this revolting land.
Or shall we play the wantons with our woes
And make some pretty match with shedding tears?
As thus: to drop them still upon one place
Till they have fretted us a pair of graves
Within the earth; and, therein laid-there lies
Two kinsmen digg'd their graves with weeping eyes.
Would not this ill do well? Well, well, I see
I talk but idly, and you laugh at me.
Most mighty prince, my Lord Northumberland,
What says King Bolingbroke? Will his Majesty
Give Richard leave to live till Richard die?
You make a leg, and Bolingbroke says ay.

NORTHUMBERLAND.
My lord, in the base court he doth attend
To speak with you; may it please you to come down?

KING RICHARD.
Down, down I come, like glist'ring Phaethon,
Wanting the manage of unruly jades.

Now what must the King do? Must I surrender? The King shall do it. Must he be overthrown? The King will be happy. Must he lose his title of King? In God's name, let it go. I'll exchange my jewels for a set of beads; my gorgeous palace for hermit's cave; my fine clothes for a beggar's gown; my ornamental goblets for a wooden dish; my sceptre for a pilgrim's walking stick; all my subjects for a pair of statues of saints, and my great kingdom for a little grave, a little little grave, an obscure grave, or I'll be buried in the king's highway, on some common trade route, where the feet of my subjects can trample over their king's head by the hour; for where I am now they are treading on my heart: once I'm buried, why not on my head? Aumerle, my tenderhearted cousin, you're weeping! We'll make a storm with hated tears; those and our sighs will beat down the summer corn, and cause a famine in this rebellious land. Or shall we be light-hearted with our sorrows, and make some pretty game with our falling tears? Like letting them all drop in one place, until they have gouged out a pair of graves for us in the earth, and we are placed within them—there lie two kinsmen who dug their graves with their own tears! Wouldn't that be funny? Well, well, I see I'm just joking, and you laugh at me. Most mighty Prince, my Lord Northumberland, what does King Bolingbroke say? Will his Majesty give Richard permission to live until Richard dies? You go and ask him, and Bolingbroke will say "yes".

My lord, he is waiting to speak with you in the lower courtyard; would you please come down?

Down, down I come, like shining Phaeton, unable to manage the unruly horses.

In the base court? Base court, where kings grow base,
To come at traitors' calls, and do them grace.
In the base court? Come down? Down, court! down, king!
For night-owls shriek where mounting larks should sing.

In the lower court? Low court, where kings become low, answering the summonses of traitors, bowing down to them In the lower court? Come down? Down, court! Down, King! Night owls are howling when ascending larks should be singing.

Exeunt from above

BOLINGBROKE.
What says his Majesty?

What does his Majesty say?

NORTHUMBERLAND.
Sorrow and grief of heart
Makes him speak fondly, like a frantic man;
Yet he is come.

Sorrow and heartfelt grief make him speak foolishly, like a madman; but he is coming.

Enter the KING, and his attendants, below

BOLINGBROKE.
Stand all apart,
And show fair duty to his Majesty. [He kneels down]
My gracious lord-

Everybody stand aside, and show due respect to his Majesty. My gracious lord—

KING RICHARD.
Fair cousin, you debase your princely knee
To make the base earth proud with kissing it.
Me rather had my heart might feel your love
Than my unpleas'd eye see your courtesy.
Up, cousin, up; your heart is up, I know,
[Touching his own head] Thus high at least, although Your
knee be low.

Fair cousin, you are insulting your princely knee by kissing the lowly earth with it. I would rather that my heart felt your love than my unimpressed eye see your formal politeness. Get up cousin, up; I know in your heart you think that you are at least as high as me, however low you bend your knees.

BOLINGBROKE.
My gracious lord, I come but for mine own.

My gracious lord, I've only come to claim what is mine.

KING RICHARD.
Your own is yours, and I am yours, and all.

You have what's yours, and I am yours, and so is everything.

BOLINGBROKE.
So far be mine, my most redoubted lord,
As my true service shall deserve your love.

I only want, my most respected lord, whatever you think I deserve for my true service.

KING RICHARD.
Well you deserve. They well deserve to have
That know the strong'st and surest way to get.
Uncle, give me your hands; nay, dry your eyes:
Tears show their love, but want their remedies.
Cousin, I am too young to be your father,
Though you are old enough to be my heir.
What you will have, I'll give, and willing too;
For do we must what force will have us do.
Set on towards London. Cousin, is it so?

You deserve much. Anyone who knows the strongest and surest way to get what they want deserves to have it. Uncle, give me your hands; no, dry your eyes: tears show love, but don't help anyone. Cousin, I am too young to be your father, although you are old enough to take my position. I'll give you whatever you want, and willingly; for I must do whatever force tells me to do. Let's march towards London. Cousin, is that what you want?

BOLINGBROKE.
Yea, my good lord.

Yes, my good lord.

KING RICHARD.
Then I must not say no.

Then I must agree.

Flourish. Exeunt

SCENE IV.

The DUKE OF YORK's garden

Enter the QUEEN and two LADIES

QUEEN.
What sport shall we devise here in this garden
To drive away the heavy thought of care?

What game shall we play here in this garden to rid ourselves of our unhappiness?

LADY.
Madam, we'll play at bowls.

Madam, we'll play at bowls.

QUEEN.
'Twill make me think the world is full of rubs
And that my fortune runs against the bias.

It will remind me that the world is full of rough spots and that my luck curves away from me.

LADY.
Madam, we'll dance.

Madam, we'll dance.

QUEEN.
My legs can keep no measure in delight,
When my poor heart no measure keeps in grief;
Therefore no dancing, girl; some other sport.

My legs cannot enjoy delightful music, when there is no music in my heart; so no dancing, girl; some other game.

LADY.
Madam, we'll tell tales.

Madam, we can tell stories.

QUEEN.
Of sorrow or of joy?

Sad ones or happy ones?

LADY.
Of either, madam.

Either sort, madam.

QUEEN.
Of neither, girl;
For if of joy, being altogether wanting,
It doth remember me the more of sorrow;
Or if of grief, being altogether had,
It adds more sorrow to my want of joy;

Neither sort, girl; a happy one would remind me of my sorrow, as I'm completely lacking in happiness; or a sad one, having a full weight of sadness, would add more sorrow

For what I have I need not to repeat,
And what I want it boots not to complain.

to my lack of happiness; I don't need to be reminded of what I have and there's no point in complaining about what I lack.

LADY.
Madam, I'll sing.

Madam, I'll sing.

QUEEN.
'Tis well' that thou hast cause;
But thou shouldst please me better wouldst thou weep.

You're lucky you have reason to; but you would please me better if you wept.

LADY.
I could weep, madam, would it do you good.

I could weep, madam, if it would do you good.

QUEEN.
And I could sing, would weeping do me good,
And never borrow any tear of thee.

And I could sing for joy, if weeping would do me any good, and I would never have to ask you to weep for me.

Enter a GARDENER and two SERVANTS

But stay, here come the gardeners.
Let's step into the shadow of these trees.
My wretchedness unto a row of pins,
They will talk of state, for every one doth so
Against a change: woe is forerun with woe.

But wait, here come the gardeners. Let's step into the shadow of these trees. I'll bet my wretchedness against a row of pins that they will talk of the state of the country, everyone does in changing times: sorrow leads to sorrow.

[QUEEN and LADIES retire]

GARDENER.
Go, bind thou up yon dangling apricocks,
Which, like unruly children, make their sire
Stoop with oppression of their prodigal weight;
Give some supportance to the bending twigs.
Go thou, and like an executioner
Cut off the heads of too fast growing sprays
That look too lofty in our commonwealth:
All must be even in our government.
You thus employ'd, I will go root away
The noisome weeds which without profit suck
The soil's fertility from wholesome flowers.

Go and tie up those dangling apricots, like badly behaved children, they make their parent bend with the strain of their terrible weight; shore up the bending twigs. Go, and like an executioner cut off the heads of the flowers which are growing too fast, that have grown too high in our kingdom: everything in our government must be level. While you're doing that, I will dig out the dirty weeds which steal away the fertility of the soil from the good flowers.

SERVANT.
Why should we, in the compass of a pale,
Keep law and form and due proportion,
Showing, as in a model, our firm estate,
When our sea-walled garden, the whole land,
Is full of weeds; her fairest flowers chok'd up,
Her fruit trees all unprun'd, her hedges ruin'd,
Her knots disordered, and her wholesome herbs
Swarming with caterpillars?

Why should we, within our fences, keep to the law, and form and proper proportions, showing our good management like a model, when our sea walled garden, the whole country, is full of weeds; her fairest flowers are overrun, her fruit trees are unpruned, her hedges are ruined, her flowerbeds in a mess, and her healthy herbs are covered with caterpillars?

GARDENER.
Hold thy peace.
He that hath suffer'd this disorder'd spring
Hath now himself met with the fall of leaf;
The weeds which his broad-spreading leaves did shelter,
That seem'd in eating him to hold him up,
Are pluck'd up root and all by Bolingbroke-
I mean the Earl of Wiltshire, Bushy, Green.

*Hold your tongue.
The one who allowed this disorder to grow has now encountered his own autumn; the weeds he sheltered under his broad spreading leaves that looked as though they were holding up as they were eating away at him, have been pulled up roots and all by Bolingbroke- I mean the Earl of Wiltshire, Bushy and Green.*

SERVANT.
What, are they dead?

What, are they dead?

GARDENER.
They are; and Bolingbroke
Hath seiz'd the wasteful King. O, what pity is it
That he had not so trimm'd and dress'd his land
As we this garden! We at time of year
Do wound the bark, the skin of our fruit trees,
Lest, being over-proud in sap and blood,
With too much riches it confound itself;
Had he done so to great and growing men,
They might have liv'd to bear, and he to taste
Their fruits of duty. Superfluous branches
We lop away, that bearing boughs may live;
Had he done so, himself had home the crown,
Which waste of idle hours hath quite thrown down.

They are; and Bolingbroke has captured the wasteful king. Oh, what a pity it is that he didn't manage his country as we manage this garden! At the right time of year we cut the bark, the skin of our fruit trees, in case its blood and sap should grow too thick, and it chokes itself with too much richness; had he done so to great and upcoming men they might have lived to produce the fruits of their service, and he could have enjoyed them. We cut away superfluous branches, so that the fruitful ones can live; if he had done that, he would still have the crown, which he has thrown away through his idleness.

SERVANT.
What, think you the King shall be deposed?

What, do you think the King will be overthrown?

GARDENER.
Depress'd he is already, and depos'd
'Tis doubt he will be. Letters came last night
To a dear friend of the good Duke of York's
That tell black tidings.

He's already been beaten, and doubtless he will be overthrown. Letters came last night to a dear friend of the good Duke of York's that contained bad news.

QUEEN.
O, I am press'd to death through want of speaking!
[Coming forward]
Thou, old Adam's likeness, set to dress this garden,
How dares thy harsh rude tongue sound this unpleasing news?
What Eve, what serpent, hath suggested thee
To make a second fall of cursed man?
Why dost thou say King Richard is depos'd?
Dar'st thou, thou little better thing than earth,
Divine his downfall? Say, where, when, and how,
Cam'st thou by this ill tidings? Speak, thou wretch.

Oh, not saying anything is killing me!

You, you copy of old Adam, told to tend this garden, how dare your harsh rude tongue speak this unpleasant news? What Eve, what snake, has suggested to you that you should make mankind fall again? Why do you say King Richard has been overthrown? Do you dare, you who is not much more than earth, predict his downfall? Tell me where, when and how, you heard this bad news. Speak, you wretch.

GARDENER.
Pardon me, madam; little joy have
To breathe this news; yet what I say is true.
King Richard, he is in the mighty hold
Of Bolingbroke. Their fortunes both are weigh'd.
In your lord's scale is nothing but himself,
And some few vanities that make him light;
But in the balance of great Bolingbroke,
Besides himself, are all the English peers,
And with that odds he weighs King Richard down.
Post you to London, and you will find it so;
I speak no more than every one doth know.

Forgive me, madam; it gives me no pleasure to speak this news; but what I say is true. King Richard is a prisoner in the firm custody of Bolingbroke. Their fortunes are balanced. On your lord's side there is only himself, and a few trifles which make him lighter; on the side of great Bolingbroke, apart from himself, are all the English peers, and with them he completely outweighs King Richard. Hurry to London, and you will find this is the case; I'm just saying what everybody knows.

QUEEN.
Nimble mischance, that art so light of foot,
Doth not thy embassage belong to me,
And am I last that knows it? O, thou thinkest
To serve me last, that I may longest keep
Thy sorrow in my breast. Come, ladies, go
To meet at London London's King in woe.
What, was I born to this, that my sad look
Should grace the triumph of great Bolingbroke?

Quick misfortune, that is so swift, wasn't your mission to come to me, and I'm the last one to know? Oh, you think you can serve me last, so I will keep your sorrow in my heart for longest. Come, ladies, we shall go and meet London's King in his sorrow in London. What, was this what I was born for, that

Gard'ner, for telling me these news of woe,
Pray God the plants thou graft'st may never grow!

my sorrow would grace the triumph of great Bolingbroke? Gardner, for telling me this sad news, I pray to God that none of your plants ever grow!

Exeunt QUEEN and LADIES

GARDENER.
Poor Queen, so that thy state might be no worse,
I would my skill were subject to thy curse.
Here did she fall a tear; here in this place
I'll set a bank of rue, sour herb of grace.
Rue, even for ruth, here shortly shall be seen,
In the remembrance of a weeping queen.

Poor Queen, if it meant your position would get no worse, I would wish for your curse to come true. She let a tear fall here; in this place I will grow a bank of rue, the sour herb of grace. Rue will shortly be seen growing here for pity, in the memory of a weeping queen.

Exeunt

ACT IV.

SCENE I.

Westminster Hall

Enter, as to the Parliament, BOLINGBROKE, AUMERLE,
NORTHUMBERLAND, PERCY,
FITZWATER, SURREY, the BISHOP OF CARLISLE, the ABBOT OF
WESTMINSTER,
and others; HERALD, OFFICERS, and BAGOT

BOLINGBROKE.
Call forth Bagot.
Now, Bagot, freely speak thy mind-
What thou dost know of noble Gloucester's death;
Who wrought it with the King, and who perform'd
The bloody office of his timeless end.

Summon Bagot.
Now, Bagot, speak openly—
what do you know about noble
Gloucester's death; who planned it with
the king, and who carried out the bloody
job of his untimely murder?

BAGOT.
Then set before my face the Lord Aumerle.

Then bring out Lord Aumerle.

BOLINGBROKE.
Cousin, stand forth, and look upon that man.

Cousin, come out, and look at that man.

BAGOT.
My Lord Aumerle, I know your daring tongue
Scorns to unsay what once it hath deliver'd.
In that dead time when Gloucester's death was plotted
I heard you say 'Is not my arm of length,
That reacheth from the restful English Court
As far as Calais, to mine uncle's head?'
Amongst much other talk that very time
I heard you say that you had rather refuse
The offer of an hundred thousand crowns
Than Bolingbroke's return to England;
Adding withal, how blest this land would be
In this your cousin's death.

My Lord Aumerle, I know your bold
tongue doesn't like to take back its words.
In that deadly time when Gloucester's
death was planned I heard you say
'Haven't I a long arm, that can reach from
the peaceful English court as far as
Calais, to kill my uncle?' Amongst many
other things said at that time I heard you
say that you would turn down an offer of
hundred thousand crowns rather than see
Bolingbroke return to England; you also
added how good the death of your cousin
would be for the country.

AUMERLE.
Princes, and noble lords,
What answer shall I make to this base man?

Princes, and noble lords,
how shall I answer this low man?

Shall I so much dishonour my fair stars
On equal terms to give him chastisement?
Either I must, or have mine honour soil'd
With the attainder of his slanderous lips.
There is my gage, the manual seal of death
That marks thee out for hell. I say thou liest,
And will maintain what thou hast said is false
In thy heart-blood, through being all too base
To stain the temper of my knightly sword.

BOLINGBROKE.
Bagot, forbear; thou shalt not take it up.

AUMERLE.
Excepting one, I would he were the best
In all this presence that hath mov'd me so.

FITZWATER.
If that thy valour stand on sympathy,
There is my gage, Aumerle, in gage to thine.
By that fair sun which shows me where thou stand'st,
I heard thee say, and vauntingly thou spak'st it,
That thou wert cause of noble Gloucester's death.
If thou deniest it twenty times, thou liest;
And I will turn thy falsehood to thy heart,
Where it was forged, with my rapier's point.

AUMERLE.
Thou dar'st not, coward, live to see that day.

FITZWATER.
Now, by my soul, I would it were this hour.

AUMERLE.
Fitzwater, thou art damn'd to hell for this.

PERCY.
Aumerle, thou liest; his honour is as true
In this appeal as thou art an unjust;
And that thou art so, there I throw my gage,
To prove it on thee to the extremest point
Of mortal breathing. Seize it, if thou dar'st.

*Shall I dishonour my noble birth so much
as to answer him back in his own terms?
I must either do that or have my honour
stained by the accusations of his
slanderous lips. There is my glove, that
seals your death that will send you to hell.
I say you are lying, and will prove this by
taking your lifeblood, although it's far too
low to stain the shining steel of my knight's
sword.*

*Bagot, hold back; you won't accept the
challenge.*

*I wish it was the best knight in this
gathering— apart from one—who had made
me so angry.*

*If your bravery depends on rank,
there is my glove, Aumerle, to match
yours. I swear by the fair sun which lights
you now, I heard you say, and say
boastingly, that you were the cause of the
death of noble Gloucester. If you deny it
twenty times, you are lying; and I will
stick the lie back into your heart, where it
was made, with the point of my sword.*

Coward, you wouldn't dare.

I swear, I wish we could do it now.

Fitzwater, you are damned to hell for this.

*Aumerle, you are lying; he is being as
honourable in this challenge as you are
being unfair; and to prove that you are
here is my glove, I shall make you answer
for it with your death. Pick it up, if you*

dare.

AUMERLE.
An if I do not, may my hands rot off
And never brandish more revengeful steel
Over the glittering helmet of my foe!

And if I don't, may my hands rot off and never again wave my revengeful sword over the glittering helmet of my enemy!

ANOTHER LORD.
I task the earth to the like, forsworn Aumerle;
And spur thee on with full as many lies
As may be halloa'd in thy treacherous ear
From sun to sun. There is my honour's pawn;
Engage it to the trial, if thou darest.

I lay down the same challenge, damned Aumerle; and encourage you with as many lies as can be shouted in your treacherous ear in the course of the day. There is my challenge; take it up, if you dare.

AUMERLE.
Who sets me else? By heaven, I'll throw at all!
I have a thousand spirits in one breast
To answer twenty thousand such as you.

Who else attacks me? By heaven, I'll have at you all! There's a thousand times more bravery in my heart than there is in twenty thousand of you.

SURREY.
My Lord Fitzwater, I do remember well
The very time Aumerle and you did talk.

My Lord Fitzwater, I remember well the exact time you and Aumerle spoke.

FITZWATER.
'Tis very true; you were in presence then,
And you can witness with me this is true.

It's very true, you were there then, and you can confirm the truth of what I say.

SURREY.
As false, by heaven, as heaven itself is true.

You are as false, by heaven, as heaven is true.

FITZWATER.
Surrey, thou liest.

Surrey, you are lying.

SURREY.
Dishonourable boy!
That lie shall lie so heavy on my sword
That it shall render vengeance and revenge
Till thou the lie-giver and that lie do lie
In earth as quiet as thy father's skull.
In proof whereof, there is my honour's pawn;
Engage it to the trial, if thou dar'st.

Dishonourable boy! My sword will give such heavy punishment for that lie that it shall hand out vengeance and revenge until you, the liar, and the lie both lie in the earth as quietly as your father's skull. As proof of that, there's my challenge; take it on, if you dare.

FITZWATER.
How fondly dost thou spur a forward horse!
If I dare eat, or drink, or breathe, or live,
I dare meet Surrey in a wilderness,
And spit upon him whilst I say he lies,
And lies, and lies. There is my bond of faith,
To tie thee to my strong correction.
As I intend to thrive in this new world,
Aumerle is guilty of my true appeal.
Besides, I heard the banish'd Norfolk say
That thou, Aumerle, didst send two of thy men
To execute the noble Duke at Calais.

How foolishly you spur on an already running horse! If I dare to eat, or drink, or breathe, or live, I will dare to meet Surrey in a wild place and spit on him whilst saying he's a liar, a liar, a liar. There is my glove, to hold you to my violent punishment. As I mean to thrive in this new order, Aumerle is as guilty as I say. Besides, I heard the exiled Norfolk say and that you, Aumerle, sent two of your men to execute the noble duke at Calais.

AUMERLE.
Some honest Christian trust me with a gage
That Norfolk lies. Here do I throw down this,
If he may be repeal'd to try his honour.

Some honest Christian lend me a glove so I can prove that Norfolk lies. I make my challenge, if he can be called back to accept it.

BOLINGBROKE.
These differences shall all rest under gage
Till Norfolk be repeal'd-repeal'd he shall be
And, though mine enemy, restor'd again
To all his lands and signories. When he is return'd,
Against Aumerle we will enforce his trial.

These arguments will all wait under the challenge until Norfolk is recalled–he shall be recalled and, although he is my enemy, he shall be given back all his lands and estates. When he comes back, he shall take up this challenge of Aumerle's.

CARLISLE.
That honourable day shall never be seen.
Many a time hath banish'd Norfolk fought
For Jesu Christ in glorious Christian field,
Streaming the ensign of the Christian cross
Against black pagans, Turks, and Saracens;
And, toil'd with works of war, retir'd himself
To Italy; and there, at Venice, gave
His body to that pleasant country's earth,
And his pure soul unto his captain, Christ,
Under whose colours he had fought so long.

That honourable day will never be seen. Many times the exiled Norfolk fought for Jesus Christ in glorious Christian battles, carrying the sign of the Christian cross against black pagans, Turks and Saracens; and, exhausted with battle, he retired to Italy; and there, at Venice, he gave his body to the pleasant earth of that country and his pure soul to his captain, Christ, for whom he had fought for so long.

BOLINGBROKE.
Why, Bishop, is Norfolk dead?

Why, Bishop, is Norfolk dead?

CARLISLE.

As surely as I live, my lord.

BOLINGBROKE.
Sweet peace conduct his sweet soul to the bosom
Of good old Abraham! Lords appellants,
Your differences shall all rest under gage
Till we assign you to your days of trial.

Enter YORK, attended

YORK.
Great Duke of Lancaster, I come to thee
From plume-pluck'd Richard, who with willing soul
Adopts thee heir, and his high sceptre yields
To the possession of thy royal hand.
Ascend his throne, descending now from him-
And long live Henry, fourth of that name!

BOLINGBROKE.
In God's name, I'll ascend the regal throne.

CARLISLE.
Marry, God forbid!
Worst in this royal presence may I speak,
Yet best beseeming me to speak the truth.
Would God that any in this noble presence
Were enough noble to be upright judge
Of noble Richard! Then true noblesse would
Learn him forbearance from so foul a wrong.
What subject can give sentence on his king?
And who sits here that is not Richard's subject?
Thieves are not judg'd but they are by to hear,
Although apparent guilt be seen in them;
And shall the figure of God's majesty,
His captain, steward, deputy elect,
Anointed, crowned, planted many years,
Be judg'd by subject and inferior breath,
And he himself not present? O, forfend it, God,
That in a Christian climate souls refin'd
Should show so heinous, black, obscene a deed!
I speak to subjects, and a subject speaks,
Stirr'd up by God, thus boldly for his king.
My Lord of Hereford here, whom you call king,
Is a foul traitor to proud Hereford's king;

As surely as I'm alive, my lord.

May his sweet soul go in peace to join
good old Abraham! You accusing lords,
all your arguments wait under their
challenges until I set a date for their trials.

Great Duke of Lancaster, I have come to
you from crestfallen Richard, who has
willingly appointed you as his heir, and he
hands his glorious sceptre into your royal
hand. Climb onto his throne, now you are
his successor– and long live Henry, fourth
king of that name!

In the name of God, I will take the royal
throne.

No, God forbid!
Although I may be the lowest ranked
person here, I may be the most suitable to
tell the truth. I wish to God that there was
anyone in this noble gathering who was
noble enough to be a fair judge of noble
Richard! Then true nobility would show
him not to commit such a terrible wrong.
What subject can pass sentence on his
king? And who is there here who is not
Richard's subject? Even thieves aren't
judged when they are absent, however
guilty they appear, so will the
representative of God's majesty, his
captain, steward, chosen deputy, anointed,
crowned, in office for many years, be
judged by his subjects and the words of his
inferiors, when he himself is not present?
Oh forbid it, God, don't let these refined
souls in a Christian country do such a
hateful, black, obscene deed! I am a
subject, speaking to subjects, inspired by

And if you crown him, let me prophesy-
The blood of English shall manure the ground,
And future ages groan for this foul act;
Peace shall go sleep with Turks and infidels,
And in this seat of peace tumultuous wars
Shall kin with kin and kind with kind confound;
Disorder, horror, fear, and mutiny,
Shall here inhabit, and this land be call'd
The field of Golgotha and dead men's skulls.
O, if you raise this house against this house,
It will the woefullest division prove
That ever fell upon this cursed earth.
Prevent it, resist it, let it not be so,
Lest child, child's children, cry against you woe.

God to speak out for his king. My Lord of Hereford here, whom you call King, is a foul traitor to the proud king of Hereford, and if you crown him, this is what I predict: the blood of the English will fertilise the ground, and future times will suffer for this foul act, peace will find its place with Turks and infidels, and, in this home of peace, terrible wars will set brother against brother, countryman against countryman. Disorder, horror, fear and mutiny will live here, and this land shall be called the plain of Golgotha, covered in dead men's skulls. Oh, if you raise this family above that one that will prove to be the deadliest division that ever fell upon this cursed earth. Prevent it, resist it, don't do it, otherwise your children and your grandchildren will cry out against you in sorrow.

NORTHUMBERLAND.
Well have you argued, sir; and, for your pains,
Of capital treason we arrest you here.
My Lord of Westminster, be it your charge
To keep him safely till his day of trial.
May it please you, lords, to grant the commons' suit?

You have argued well, sir; and, for your efforts, I arrest you on a charge of capital treason. My Lord of Westminster, make it your duty to keep him safe until the day of his trial. Do you agree, my lords, to grant the request of the Commons?

BOLINGBROKE.
Fetch hither Richard, that in common view
He may surrender; so we shall proceed
Without suspicion.

Bring Richard here, so that he can surrender in open view; that way we can proceed without any suspicion.

YORK.
I will be his conduct.

I shall bring him here.

Exit

BOLINGBROKE.
Lords, you that here are under our arrest,
Procure your sureties for your days of answer.
Little are we beholding to your love,
And little look'd for at your helping hands.

Lords, you who are here under my arrest, find your bail against the day of your trial. I owe little to your love, and I didn't ask you for much help.

Re-enter YORK, with KING RICHARD, and OFFICERS

bearing the regalia

KING RICHARD.
Alack, why am I sent for to a king,
Before I have shook off the regal thoughts
Wherewith I reign'd? I hardly yet have learn'd
To insinuate, flatter, bow, and bend my knee.
Give sorrow leave awhile to tutor me
To this submission. Yet I well remember
The favours of these men. Were they not mine?
Did they not sometime cry 'All hail!' to me?
So Judas did to Christ; but he, in twelve,
Found truth in all but one; I, in twelve thousand, none.
God save the King! Will no man say amen?
Am I both priest and clerk? Well then, amen.
God save the King! although I be not he;
And yet, amen, if heaven do think him me.
To do what service am I sent for hither?

Alas, why have I been summoned by a King before I have thrown off the royal habits I had when I ruled? I have hardly learned yet to manoeuvre, flatter, bow, and bend my knee. Give sorrow time to teach me how to be so submissive. But I clearly remember the faces of these men. Weren't they mine? Didn't they sometimes call out 'We salute you!' to me? That's what Judas did to Christ; but out of twelve men all but one were loyal to him; out of twelve thousand I don't have one. God save the King! Will no man agree to that? Do I have to be the priest and the responder? Well then, amen. God save the King! Although I am not him; and yet, amen, if heaven thinks I am. What have you summoned me for?

YORK.
To do that office of thine own good will
Which tired majesty did make thee offer-
The resignation of thy state and crown
To Henry Bolingbroke.

To willingly perform the task which you offered through your royal exhaustion—tohand over your country and your crown to Henry Bolingbroke.

KING RICHARD.
Give me the crown. Here, cousin, seize the crown.
Here, cousin,
On this side my hand, and on that side thine.
Now is this golden crown like a deep well
That owes two buckets, filling one another;
The emptier ever dancing in the air,
The other down, unseen, and full of water.
That bucket down and full of tears am I,
Drinking my griefs, whilst you mount up on high.

*Give me the crown. Here, cousin, take the crown. Here, cousin,
my hand is on this side, yours on that. Now this golden crown is like a deep well that has two buckets, filling each other; the empty one always swinging in the air, the other low down, unseen, and full of water. I am the lower bucket, full of tears, drowning in grief, while you climb up high.*

BOLINGBROKE.
I thought you had been willing to resign.

I thought you were willing to resign.

KING RICHARD.
My crown I am; but still my griefs are mine.
You may my glories and my state depose,

Yes, to resign my crown; but my sorrows are still mine. You may overthrow my

But not my griefs; still am I king of those.

glory and my position, but not my sorrows; I'm still king of those.

BOLINGBROKE.
Part of your cares you give me with your crown.

You hand some of your cares to me with your crown.

KING RICHARD.
Your cares set up do not pluck my cares down.
My care is loss of care, by old care done;
Your care is gain of care, by new care won.
The cares I give I have, though given away;
They tend the crown, yet still with me they stay.

You taking on cares does not take them from me. My sorrow is that I have lost care by finishing with old cares; your sorrow is that you've gained care, being loaded with new cares. The cares I give away still stay with me; they go with the crown, but they stay with me.

BOLINGBROKE.
Are you contented to resign the crown?

Are you content to resign the crown?

KING RICHARD.
Ay, no; no, ay; for I must nothing be;
Therefore no no, for I resign to thee.
Now mark me how I will undo myself:
I give this heavy weight from off my head,
And this unwieldy sceptre from my hand,
The pride of kingly sway from out my heart;
With mine own tears I wash away my balm,
With mine own hands I give away my crown,
With mine own tongue deny my sacred state,
With mine own breath release all duteous oaths;
All pomp and majesty I do forswear;
My manors, rents, revenues, I forgo;
My acts, decrees, and statutes, I deny.
God pardon all oaths that are broke to me!
God keep all vows unbroke are made to thee!
Make me, that nothing have, with nothing griev'd,
And thou with all pleas'd, that hast an achiev'd.
Long mayst thou live in Richard's seat to sit,
And soon lie Richard in an earthly pit.
God save King Henry, unking'd Richard says,
And send him many years of sunshine days!
What more remains?

Yes, no; no, yes; for I must be nothing; therefore no 'no', for I resign to you. Now, see how I undermine myself. I give you this heavy weight from off my head, and this clumsy sceptre from my hand, the pride of royal power from out of my heart; I wash away the anointing oil with my tears, with my own hands I give you my crown, with my own tongue I reject my holy position, with my own breath I release all who have sworn oaths to me; I give up all ceremony and majesty; I give up my manors, rents and revenues; I reject all my acts, decrees and statutes. May God pardon all the promises to me that have been broken, and keep all the promises that are made to you unbroken! Make me, who has nothing, be grieved with nothing, and may you who has won everything be pleased with everything. May you live long sitting in Richard's seat, and soon bury Richard in his grave. God save King Henry, no longer king Richard says, and give him many years of sunny days! What is left?

NORTHUMBERLAND.
No more; but that you read
These accusations, and these grievous crimes
Committed by your person and your followers
Against the state and profit of this land;
That, by confessing them, the souls of men
May deem that you are worthily depos'd.

That's enough; all you need to do now is read out these accusations, these grievous crimes committed by you and your followers against the state and best interest of this land; so that men, hearing you confess to them can judge that you are rightly overthrown.

KING RICHARD.
Must I do so? And must I ravel out
My weav'd-up follies? Gentle Northumberland,
If thy offences were upon record,
Would it not shame thee in so fair a troop
To read a lecture of them? If thou wouldst,
There shouldst thou find one heinous article,
Containing the deposing of a king
And cracking the strong warrant of an oath,
Mark'd with a blot, damn'd in the book of heaven.
Nay, all of you that stand and look upon me
Whilst that my wretchedness doth bait myself,
Though some of you, with Pilate, wash your hands,
Showing an outward pity-yet you Pilates
Have here deliver'd me to my sour cross,
And water cannot wash away your sin.

Do I have to? And must I unravel all my intertwined foolishness? Sweet Northumberland, if everything you've done wrong was written down, wouldn't you be ashamed to read them out in such fair company? If you did you would find one awful item there concerning the overthrow of a king and the breaking of a strong oath, marked with a blot, damned in the book of heaven. No, all of you who stand looking at me as I am tormented with my wretchedness, although some of you, like Pilate, wash your hands and pretend to show pity—yet you Pilates have delivered me to my bitter cross, and water cannot wash away your sins.

NORTHUMBERLAND.
My lord, dispatch; read o'er these
articles.

My Lord, get it over with; read these articles.

KING RICHARD.
Mine eyes are full of tears; I cannot see.
And yet salt water blinds them not so much
But they can see a sort of traitors here.
Nay, if I turn mine eyes upon myself,
I find myself a traitor with the rest;
For I have given here my soul's consent
T'undeck the pompous body of a king;
Made glory base, and sovereignty a slave,
Proud majesty a subject, state a peasant.

My eyes are full of tears; I cannot see. And yet the salt water does not make them so blind that they cannot see this group of traitors here. No, if I take a look at myself I find I am a traitor with the rest of them; for I have here given my agreement to take away the ceremonial robes of a king; I have made glory low, and royalty a slave, proud majesty a subject, my state a peasant.

NORTHUMBERLAND.
My lord-

My lord–

KING RICHARD.
No lord of thine, thou haught insulting man,
Nor no man's lord; I have no name, no tide-
No, not that name was given me at the font-
But 'tis usurp'd. Alack the heavy day,
That I have worn so many winters out,
And know not now what name to call myself!
O that I were a mockery king of snow,
Standing before the sun of Bolingbroke
To melt myself away in water drops!
Good king, great king, and yet not greatly good,
An if my word be sterling yet in England,
Let it command a mirror hither straight,
That it may show me what a face I have
Since it is bankrupt of his majesty.

No lord of yours, you haughty insulting man; no man's lord. I have no name, no title; no, not even that name that was given to me at my christening, it has been stolen. What a terrible thing, that I have reached such an age and now don't know what name to call myself! I wish I was a fake king made of snow, standing under the sun of Bolingbroke, so that I could melt away in drops of water! Good King, great King, though not greatly good, if my words still have any power in England, let me order a mirror to be brought here at once, so it can show me what my face looks like now it has lost its majesty.

BOLINGBROKE.
Go some of you and fetch a looking-glass.

Some of you go and fetch a looking glass.

Exit an attendant

NORTHUMBERLAND.
Read o'er this paper while the glass doth come.

Read out this paper while we're waiting for the mirror.

KING RICHARD.
Fiend, thou torments me ere I come to hell.

You devil, you torture me before I get to hell.

BOLINGBROKE.
Urge it no more, my Lord Northumberland.

Stop asking him, my Lord Northumberland.

NORTHUMBERLAND.
The Commons will not, then, be satisfied.

The Commons will not be satisfied if he doesn't read it.

KING RICHARD.
They shall be satisfied. I'll read enough,
When I do see the very book indeed
Where all my sins are writ, and that's myself.

They will be satisfied. I will read enough when I have seen the very book where my sins are written, and that is my face.

Re-enter attendant with glass

Give me that glass, and therein will I read.
No deeper wrinkles yet? Hath sorrow struck
So many blows upon this face of mine
And made no deeper wounds? O flatt'ring glass,
Like to my followers in prosperity,
Thou dost beguile me! Was this face the face
That every day under his household roof
Did keep ten thousand men? Was this the face
That like the sun did make beholders wink?
Is this the face which fac'd so many follies
That was at last out-fac'd by Bolingbroke?
A brittle glory shineth in this face;
As brittle as the glory is the face;
[Dashes the glass against the ground]
For there it is, crack'd in a hundred shivers.
Mark, silent king, the moral of this sport-
How soon my sorrow hath destroy'd my face.

Give me that mirror, and I will read from it. No deeper wrinkles yet? Has sorrow struck so many blows upon my face and not made deeper wounds? Oh flattering glass, like my followers when I was fortunate, you are deceiving me. Was this the face that managed to keep ten thousand men as part of his household? Was this the face that made onlookers squint as if looking at the sun? Is this the face which committed so many follies and was at last stared down by Bolingbroke? There is a brittle glory shining in this face; this face is as brittle as glory, for there it is, smashed into a hundred splinters. Make a note, silent King, of the moral of this— see how quickly my sorrow destroyed my face.

BOLINGBROKE.
The shadow of your sorrow hath destroy'd
The shadow of your face.

The imitation of your sorrow has destroyed the imitation of your face.

KING RICHARD.
Say that again.
The shadow of my sorrow? Ha! let's see.
'Tis very true: my grief lies all within;
And these external manner of laments
Are merely shadows to the unseen grief
That swells with silence in the tortur'd soul.
There lies the substance; and I thank thee, king,
For thy great bounty, that not only giv'st
Me cause to wail, but teachest me the way
How to lament the cause. I'll beg one boon,
And then be gone and trouble you no more.
Shall I obtain it?

*Say that again.
The imitation of my sorrow? Hah! Let's see. It's very true: all my sorrow is within; all these external laments are just imitations of the unseen sorrow that swells in silence inside the tortured soul. There is the substance of it; and I thank you, King, for your great gift, not only giving me reason to be sad, but showing me the way to mourn for it. I'll ask you one favour, and then I shall be gone and give you no more trouble. Will you grant it?*

BOLINGBROKE.
Name it, fair cousin.

Name it, fair cousin.

KING RICHARD.
Fair cousin! I am greater than a king;
For when I was a king, my flatterers
Were then but subjects; being now a subject,
I have a king here to my flatterer.

Fair cousin! I am greater than a king; for when I was a king, my flatterers were just my subjects; now I am a subject, I have a king here as my flatterer.

Being so great, I have no need to beg.

Being so great, I don't need to beg.

BOLINGBROKE.
Yet ask.

Just ask.

KING RICHARD.
And shall I have?

And shall I have it?

BOLINGBROKE.
You shall.

You shall.

KING RICHARD.
Then give me leave to go.

Then let me leave.

BOLINGBROKE.
Whither?

To go where?

KING RICHARD.
Whither you will, so I were from your sights.

Wherever you want, to get me out of your sight.

BOLINGBROKE.
Go, some of you convey him to the Tower.

Go, some of you escort him to the Tower.

KING RICHARD.
O, good! Convey! Conveyers are you all,
That rise thus nimbly by a true king's fall.

O, good! Escort! You are all escorts, all swiftly promoted due to the fall of a true king.

Exeunt KING RICHARD, some Lords and a Guard

BOLINGBROKE.
On Wednesday next we solemnly set down
Our coronation. Lords, prepare yourselves.

I set aside next Wednesday for my solemn coronation. Lords, make your preparations.

Exeunt all but the ABBOT OF WESTMINSTER, the
BISHOP OF CARLISLE, and AUMERLE

ABBOT.
A woeful pageant have we here beheld.

We have seen a sorry sight here.

CARLISLE.
The woe's to come; the children yet unborn
Shall feel this day as sharp to them as thorn.

The sorrow is yet to come; children not yet born will suffer as a result of today's

AUMERLE.
You holy clergymen, is there no plot
To rid the realm of this pernicious blot?

ABBOT.
My lord,
Before I freely speak my mind herein,
You shall not only take the sacrament
To bury mine intents, but also to effect
Whatever I shall happen to devise.
I see your brows are full of discontent,
Your hearts of sorrow, and your eyes of tears.
Come home with me to supper; I will lay
A plot shall show us all a merry day.

Exeunt

events.

*You holy clergymen, don't you have a way
to remove this stain from the country?*

*My lord,
before I freely speak my mind about that,
you will not only swear by the sacrament
that you will keep my plans secret, but
also that you will do whatever I invent.
I see that you are frowning in anger,
your heart is full of sorrow, and your eyes
are full of tears. Come home with me to
supper; I will outline a plot which will
make us all happy.*

ACT V.

SCENE 1.

London. A street leading to the Tower

Enter the QUEEN, with her attendants

QUEEN.
This way the King will come; this is the way
To Julius Caesar's ill-erected tower,
To whose flint bosom my condemned lord
Is doom'd a prisoner by proud Bolingbroke.
Here let us rest, if this rebellious earth
Have any resting for her true King's queen.

The king will come this way; this is the way to Julius Caesar's evil tower, to which my condemned lord has been sent as a prisoner by haughty Bolingbroke. Let's rest here, if there is any rest anywhere on this rebellious earth for the queen of a true King.

Enter KING RICHARD and Guard

But soft, but see, or rather do not see,
My fair rose wither. Yet look up, behold,
That you in pity may dissolve to dew,
And wash him fresh again with true-love tears.
Ah, thou, the model where old Troy did stand;
Thou map of honour, thou King Richard's tomb,
And not King Richard; thou most beauteous inn,
Why should hard-favour'd grief be lodg'd in thee,
When triumph is become an alehouse guest?

But look, or rather don't look, there is my fair rose withered. But look up, look, you who dissolve into pity like dew, and wash him clean again with the tears of true love. Ah, you, you are like the ruins of old Troy; you model of honour, you tomb of King Richard, you are not King Richard; you beautiful inn, why should hard faced grief visit you, when triumph visits every common alehouse?

KING RICHARD.
Join not with grief, fair woman, do not so,
To make my end too sudden. Learn, good soul,
To think our former state a happy dream;
From which awak'd, the truth of what we are
Shows us but this: I am sworn brother, sweet,
To grim Necessity; and he and
Will keep a league till death. Hie thee to France,
And cloister thee in some religious house.
Our holy lives must win a new world's crown,
Which our profane hours here have thrown down.

Don't grieve so, fair woman, do not write me off so soon. Learn, good soul, to think of our former position as a happy dream; having woken up, we can see the truth of what we are: I am the sworn brother, my sweet, of grim necessity; and he and I will be together until death. Take yourself to France, and retreat into some religious house. We must work to win a new crown in heaven, as we have lost the one we had on earth.

QUEEN.

What, is my Richard both in shape and mind
Transform'd and weak'ned? Hath Bolingbroke depos'd
Thine intellect? Hath he been in thy heart?
The lion dying thrusteth forth his paw
And wounds the earth, if nothing else, with rage
To be o'erpow'r'd; and wilt thou, pupil-like,
Take the correction mildly, kiss the rod,
And fawn on rage with base humility,
Which art a lion and the king of beasts?

What, has my Richard been transformed and weakened both in body and mind? Has Bolingbroke overthrown your intellect? Has he been in your heart? The dying lion puts out his paw and wounds the earth, if nothing else, with rage at his downfall; are you going to be like a schoolboy, taking your punishment mildly, kissing the cane, and bow down to rage with low humbleness, you who are a lion and the king of beasts?

KING RICHARD.
A king of beasts, indeed! If aught but beasts,
I had been still a happy king of men.
Good sometimes queen, prepare thee hence for France.
Think I am dead, and that even here thou takest,
As from my death-bed, thy last living leave.
In winter's tedious nights sit by the fire
With good old folks, and let them tell thee tales
Of woeful ages long ago betid;
And ere thou bid good night, to quit their griefs
Tell thou the lamentable tale of me,
And send the hearers weeping to their beds;
For why, the senseless brands will sympathize
The heavy accent of thy moving tongue,
And in compassion weep the fire out;
And some will mourn in ashes, some coal-black,
For the deposing of a rightful king.

A king of beasts, indeed! If it had only been of beasts, I would still be a happy king of men. My good once upon a time Queen, go to France. Imagine that I am dead, and that even now you are making your last living farewell to me, as if you were at my deathbed. In the dull nights of winter sit by the fire with good old people, and let them tell you stories of sad things which happened long ago; and before you say good night, to cap their sorry tales tell them of my sad story, and send the listeners off weeping to their beds; because the unfeeling sticks will sympathise with the heavy words your tongue shall speak, and out of pity they will put out the fire; and some will mourn with ashes, black as coal, the overthrow of a rightful king.

Enter NORTHUMBERLAND attended

NORTHUMBERLAND.
My lord, the mind of Bolingbroke is chang'd;
You must to Pomfret, not unto the Tower.
And, madam, there is order ta'en for you:
With all swift speed you must away to France.

My lord, Bolingbroke has changed his mind; you must go to Pomfret, not to the tower. And, madam, arrangements have been made for you: you must go as quickly as possible to France.

KING RICHARD.
Northumberland, thou ladder wherewithal
The mounting Bolingbroke ascends my throne,
The time shall not be many hours of age

Northumberland, you ladder with which the climbing Bolingbroke gets onto my throne, it won't be very far in the future

More than it is, ere foul sin gathering head
Shall break into corruption. Thou shalt think
Though he divide the realm and give thee half
It is too little, helping him to all;
And he shall think that thou, which knowest the way
To plant unrightful kings, wilt know again,
Being ne'er so little urg'd, another way
To pluck him headlong from the usurped throne.
The love of wicked men converts to fear;
That fear to hate; and hate turns one or both
To worthy danger and deserved death.

before foul sin gathers pace and explodes into destruction. Even if he splits the kingdom and gives you half you will think it is too little, since you helped him to get the whole thing; and he shall think that you, who knows the way to install kings who have no right to be there, will, with just a little provocation, know how to find a way of throwing him headlong from his stolen throne. The love of wicked men converts itself to fear, fear turns to hate, and that hate brings one or both the danger and death they deserve.

NORTHUMBERLAND.
My guilt be on my head, and there an end.
Take leave, and part; for you must part forthwith.

I take responsibility for my guilt, that's the end of it. Say goodbye, and go; you must part at once.

KING RICHARD.
Doubly divorc'd! Bad men, you violate
A twofold marriage-'twixt my crown and me,
And then betwixt me and my married wife.
Let me unkiss the oath 'twixt thee and me;
And yet not so, for with a kiss 'twas made.
Part us, Northumberland; I towards the north,
Where shivering cold and sickness pines the clime;
My wife to France, from whence set forth in pomp,
She came adorned hither like sweet May,
Sent back like Hallowmas or short'st of day.

Divorced twice! Bad men, you have broken two marriages–the one between me and my crown, and then the one between me and my married wife. Let me kiss away the promise between you and me; and yet I can't, because it was made with a kiss. Pull us apart, Northumberland; I go north, where shivering cold and disease fills the air; my wife goes to France, from where she set out with great ceremony, when she came here she was like a sweet May day, she is sent back like Halloween or the shortest day.

QUEEN.
And must we be divided? Must we part?

And must we be split up? Must we part?

KING RICHARD.
Ay, hand from hand, my love, and heart from heart.

Yes my love, hand from hand and heart from heart.

QUEEN.
Banish us both, and send the King with me.

Banish us both, and send the King with me.

NORTHUMBERLAND.

That were some love, but little policy.

That would show love, but not sense.

QUEEN.
Then whither he goes thither let me go.

Then let me go with him.

KING RICHARD.
So two, together weeping, make one woe.
Weep thou for me in France, I for thee here;
Better far off than near, be ne'er the near.
Go, count thy way with sighs; I mine with groans.

So two, weeping together, make one sorrow. You weep for me in France, I shall weep for you here; better to be far apart than close but not close enough. Go, measure your journey with sighs; I shall measure mine with groans.

QUEEN.
So longest way shall have the longest moans.

So the longest journey will have the longest moans.

KING RICHARD.
Twice for one step I'll groan, the way being short,
And piece the way out with a heavy heart.
Come, come, in wooing sorrow let's be brief,
Since, wedding it, there is such length in grief.
One kiss shall stop our mouths, and dumbly part;
Thus give I mine, and thus take I thy heart.

As I'm going the shortest way, I will groan twice with every step, and measure my way with a heavy heart. Come, come, let's be brief in our wooing of sorrow, as when we marry it our grief will be so long. Close our mouths with one kiss, and part in silence; so I give you mine, and I take your heart.

QUEEN.
Give me mine own again; 'twere no good part
To take on me to keep and kill thy heart.
So, now I have mine own again, be gone,
That I may strive to kill it with a groan.

Give me mine back; it's not fair to ask me to keep and kill your heart. So, I have my own back, now go, so that I can try to kill it with a groan.

KING RICHARD.
We make woe wanton with this fond delay.
Once more, adieu; the rest let sorrow say.

We are making sorrow grow with this tender foolish delay. Once more, goodbye; let sorrow say the rest.

Exeunt

SCENE II.

The DUKE OF YORK's palace

Enter the DUKE OF YORK and the DUCHESS

DUCHESS.
My Lord, you told me you would tell the rest,
When weeping made you break the story off,
Of our two cousins' coming into London.

My lord, you told me you would tell me the rest of the story of our cousins' arrival in London, when your weeping made you break off the story.

YORK.
Where did I leave?

How far had I got?

DUCHESS.
At that sad stop, my lord,
Where rude misgoverned hands from windows' tops
Threw dust and rubbish on King Richard's head.

To that sad point, my lord, when vulgar badly ruled hands threw dust and rubbish on King Richard's head from their windows.

YORK.
Then, as I said, the Duke, great Bolingbroke,
Mounted upon a hot and fiery steed
Which his aspiring rider seem'd to know,
With slow but stately pace kept on his course,
Whilst all tongues cried 'God save thee, Bolingbroke!'
You would have thought the very windows spake,
So many greedy looks of young and old
Through casements darted their desiring eyes
Upon his visage; and that all the walls
With painted imagery had said at once
'Jesu preserve thee! Welcome, Bolingbroke!'
Whilst he, from the one side to the other turning,
Bareheaded, lower than his proud steed's neck,
Bespake them thus, 'I thank you, countrymen.'
And thus still doing, thus he pass'd along.

Then, as I said, the Duke, great Bolingbroke, mounted on a hot and fiery horse which seemed to sympathise with its aspiring rider, kept on his way with a slow but regal pace, while everybody cried 'God save you, Bolingbroke!' You would have thought the windows themselves were speaking, so many, both young and old, greedily wanted to get a glimpse of his face; you would have thought all the walls were covered with posters which all read 'Jesus save you! Welcome, Bolingbroke!' Meanwhile he, turning from one side to the other, bareheaded, bowed lower than the neck of his proud horse, spoke these words, 'I thank you, countrymen.' And so he did this and moved along.

DUCHESS.
Alack, poor Richard! where rode he the whilst?

Alas, poor Richard! Where was he riding

YORK.
As in a theatre the eyes of men
After a well-grac'd actor leaves the stage
Are idly bent on him that enters next,
Thinking his prattle to be tedious;
Even so, or with much more contempt, men's eyes
Did scowl on gentle Richard; no man cried 'God save
him!'
No joyful tongue gave him his welcome home;
But dust was thrown upon his sacred head;
Which with such gentle sorrow he shook off,
His face still combating with tears and smiles,
The badges of his grief and patience,
That had not God, for some strong purpose, steel'd
The hearts of men, they must perforce have melted,
And barbarism itself have pitied him.
But heaven hath a hand in these events,
To whose high will we bound our calm contents.
To Bolingbroke are we sworn subjects now,
Whose state and honour I for aye allow.

DUCHESS.
Here comes my son Aumerle.

YORK.
Aumerle that was
But that is lost for being Richard's friend,
And madam, you must call him Rutland now.
I am in Parliament pledge for his truth
And lasting fealty to the new-made king.

Enter AUMERLE

DUCHESS.
Welcome, my son. Who are the violets now
That strew the green lap of the new come spring?

AUMERLE.
Madam, I know not, nor I greatly care not.
God knows I had as lief be none as one.

while this was going on?

It was as if in a theatre when a skilful actor leaves the stage, and the audience glances at the one who comes on next, finding his prattle tedious; that was how, or with even more contempt, men scowled on gentle Richard; no man cried 'God save him!' No happy tongue welcomed him home; but dust was thrown upon his sacred head; which he shook off with such gentle sadness, his face alternating between tears and smiles, the signs of his sorrow and endurance, that if God had not, for some great purpose, hardened the hearts of men, they would surely have melted, and even barbarians would have pitied him. But heaven orders these events, and we must be happy to follow them. We are now sworn subjects of Bolingbroke, and I now recognise his position.

Here comes my son Aumerle.

He was Aumerle, but he has lost his title for being Richard's friend, and madam, you must now call him Rutland. I have sworn to his loyalty in Parliament and promised that he will follow the newly created king.

Welcome, my son. Who are the violets which now cover the green fields of this new spring?

Madam, I don't know, nor do I much care. God knows I don't care if I'm one or not.

YORK.
Well, bear you well in this new spring of time,
Lest you be cropp'd before you come to prime.
What news from Oxford? Do these justs and triumphs
hold?

Well, behave yourself well in this new springtime, so that you won't be cut down before your prime. What news from Oxford? Are they still having these jousts and processions?

AUMERLE.
For aught I know, my lord, they do.

For all I know, my lord, they are.

YORK.
You will be there, I know.

I know you will be there.

AUMERLE.
If God prevent not, I purpose so.

If God doesn't stop me, I intend to be.

YORK.
What seal is that that hangs without thy bosom?
Yea, look'st thou pale? Let me see the writing.

What's that seal that's hanging outside your shirt? Why are you looking pale? Let me see the writing.

AUMERLE.
My lord, 'tis nothing.

My Lord, it's nothing.

YORK.
No matter, then, who see it.
I will be satisfied; let me see the writing.

It doesn't matter who sees it then. You will do as I say; let me see the writing.

AUMERLE.
I do beseech your Grace to pardon me;
It is a matter of small consequence
Which for some reasons I would not have seen.

I beg your Grace to excuse me; it's a matter of little importance which for some reasons I don't want to be seen.

YORK.
Which for some reasons, sir, I mean to see.
I fear, I fear-

And for some reasons, sir, I intend to see it. I fear, I fear—

DUCHESS.
What should you fear?
'Tis nothing but some bond that he is ent'red into
For gay apparel 'gainst the triumph-day.

Why should you fear? It's nothing but some loan agreement he's taken out for flashy clothes on the day of the triumph.

YORK.
Bound to himself! What doth he with a bond
That he is bound to? Wife, thou art a fool.
Boy, let me see the writing.

Has he made an agreement with himself? What would he be doing with his own bond? Wife, you are a fool. Boy, let me see the writing.

AUMERLE.
I do beseech you, pardon me; I may not show it.

I beg you to excuse me; I can't show it.

YORK.
I will be satisfied; let me see it, I say.
[He plucks it out of his bosom, and reads it]
Treason, foul treason! Villain! traitor! slave!

I will be obeyed; let me see it, I say.

Treason, foul treason! Villain! Traitor! Slave!

DUCHESS.
What is the matter, my lord?

What is the matter, my lord?

YORK.
Ho! who is within there?

Hello! Who's in there?

Enter a servant

Saddle my horse.
God for his mercy, what treachery is here!

Saddle my horse.
May God have mercy, what treachery this is!

DUCHESS.
Why, York, what is it, my lord?

Why, York, what is it, my lord?

YORK.
Give me my boots, I say; saddle my horse.
Exit servant
Now, by mine honour, by my life, my troth,
I will appeach the villain.

Give me my boots, I say; saddle my horse.

Now, on my honour, by my life, my oath, I will impeach the villain.

DUCHESS.
What is the matter?

What is the matter?

YORK.
Peace, foolish woman.

Be quiet, stupid woman.

DUCHESS.
I will not peace. What is the matter, Aumerle?

I won't be quiet. What is the matter, Aumerle?

AUMERLE.
Good mother, be content; it is no more
Than my poor life must answer.

*Good mother, be content; it's only
a matter of my life.*

DUCHESS.
Thy life answer!

Your life!

YORK.
Bring me my boots. I will unto the King.

Bring me my boots. I shall go to the king.

His man enters with his boots

DUCHESS.
Strike him, Aumerle. Poor boy, thou art amaz'd.
Hence, villain! never more come in my sight.

*Strike him, Aumerle. Poor boy, you are
stupefied. Get out, villain! I never want
to see you again.*

YORK.
Give me my boots, I say.

Give me my boots, I say.

DUCHESS.
Why, York, what wilt thou do?
Wilt thou not hide the trespass of thine own?
Have we more sons? or are we like to have?
Is not my teeming date drunk up with time?
And wilt thou pluck my fair son from mine age
And rob me of a happy mother's name?
Is he not like thee? Is he not thine own?

*Why, York, what are you doing?
Will you not hide the misdemeanours of
your own family? Have we more sons?
Or are we likely to have? Hasn't my time
for breeding run out? Will you steal my
fair son away from my old age and take
away my title of a happy mother?
Isn't he like you? Isn't he yours?*

YORK.
Thou fond mad woman,
Wilt thou conceal this dark conspiracy?
A dozen of them here have ta'en the sacrament,
And interchangeably set down their hands
To kill the King at Oxford.

*You stupid mad woman,
do you want to hide this conspiracy?
A dozen of them have here taken
a holy oath that they will
kill the King at Oxford.*

DUCHESS.
He shall be none;
We'll keep him here. Then what is that to him?

*He won't be one of them;
we'll keep him here. Then what does it
matter?*

YORK.
Away, fond woman! were he twenty times my son
I would appeach him.

*Get off, foolish woman! If he were my son
twenty times over I would still inform on
him.*

DUCHESS.
Hadst thou groan'd for him
As I have done, thou wouldst be more pitiful.
But now I know thy mind: thou dost suspect
That I have been disloyal to thy bed
And that he is a bastard, not thy son.
Sweet York, sweet husband, be not of that mind.
He is as like thee as a man may be
Not like to me, or any of my kin,
And yet I love him.

If you had had the pain of his labour as I have, you would show more pity. But now I know what you think: you suspect that I have been adulterous and now he is a bastard, not your son. Sweet York, sweet husband, don't think that. He's like you as any man could be, he doesn't resemble me, or any of my family, and yet I love him.

YORK.
Make way, unruly woman!

Out of the way, rebellious woman!

Exit

DUCHESS.
After, Aumerle! Mount thee upon his horse;
Spur post, and get before him to the King,
And beg thy pardon ere he do accuse thee.
I'll not be long behind; though I be old,
I doubt not but to ride as fast as York;
And never will I rise up from the ground
Till Bolingbroke have pardon'd thee. Away, be gone.

Follow him, Aumerle! Take his horse; ride as fast as you can and get to the King before him, and ask for his pardon before you are accused. I won't be far behind; although I am old, I back myself to ride as fast as York; and I will never get off my knees until Bolingbroke has pardoned you. Go, go.

Exeunt

SCENE III.

Windsor Castle

Enter BOLINGBROKE as King, PERCY, and other LORDS

BOLINGBROKE.
Can no man tell me of my unthrifty son?
'Tis full three months since I did see him last.
If any plague hang over us, 'tis he.
I would to God, my lords, he might be found.
Inquire at London, 'mongst the taverns there,
For there, they say, he daily doth frequent
With unrestrained loose companions,
Even such, they say, as stand in narrow lanes
And beat our watch and rob our passengers,
Which he, young wanton and effeminate boy,
Takes on the point of honour to support
So dissolute a crew.

Can't anyone tell me about my profligate son? It's fully three moths since I last saw him. If there's any curse hanging over me it's him. I wish to God, my lords, that he could be found. Ask in London, in the taverns there, for they say he goes to them daily with lawless vulgar companions, the type, they say, who stand in alleyways and beat the watchmen and rob travellers, and he, lusty and unmanly youth, thinks it is a point of honour to support such a dissipated crew.

PERCY.
My lord, some two days since I saw the Prince,
And told him of those triumphs held at Oxford.

My Lord, I saw the Prince some two days ago, and told him of the triumphs to be held at Oxford.

BOLINGBROKE.
And what said the gallant?

And what did the brave lad say?

PERCY.
His answer was, he would unto the stews,
And from the common'st creature pluck a glove
And wear it as a favour; and with that
He would unhorse the lustiest challenger.

He said that he would go into the slums, and take a glove from the lowest creature there and wear it as a favour; and in that way he would unseat the strongest challenger.

BOLINGBROKE.
As dissolute as desperate; yet through both
I see some sparks of better hope, which elder years
May happily bring forth. But who comes here?

As dissipated as he is desperate; but I can see through those qualities to see a better hope, which age may happily bring to fruition. But who is this?

109

Enter AUMERLE amazed

AUMERLE.
Where is the King?

Where is the King?

BOLINGBROKE.
What means our cousin that he stares and looks
So wildly?

*Why is our cousin staring and looking
so wild?*

AUMERLE.
God save your Grace! I do beseech your Majesty,
To have some conference with your Grace alone.

*God save your Grace! I beg your Majesty
to let me speak with you in private.*

BOLINGBROKE.
Withdraw yourselves, and leave us here alone.

Withdraw, and leave us alone.

Exeunt PERCY and LORDS

What is the matter with our cousin now?

What is the problem with you, cousin?

AUMERLE.
For ever may my knees grow to the earth,
[Kneels]
My tongue cleave to my roof within my mouth,
Unless a pardon ere I rise or speak.

*May my knees never leave the earth,
may my tongue become stuck to the roof of
my mouth, unless I'm given a pardon
before I get up or speak.*

BOLINGBROKE.
Intended or committed was this fault?
If on the first, how heinous e'er it be,
To win thy after-love I pardon thee.

*Is your fault something you have planned
or something you've done? If it's the first,
however awful it is, to win your love
hereafter I pardon you.*

AUMERLE.
Then give me leave that I may turn the key,
That no man enter till my tale be done.

*Then give me permission to lock the door,
so that no man can come in until I have
told my story.*

BOLINGBROKE.
Have thy desire.

Do as you wish.

[The DUKE OF YORK knocks at the door and crieth]

YORK.
[Within] My liege, beware; look to thyself;
Thou hast a traitor in thy presence there.

*Look out, my lord; guard yourself;
you have a traitor in there with you.*

BOLINGBROKE.
[Drawing] Villain, I'll make thee safe.

Villain, I'll finish you.

AUMERLE.
Stay thy revengeful hand; thou hast no cause to fear.

Stop your revenging hand; you have no reason to fear.

YORK.
[Within] Open the door, secure, foolhardy King.
Shall I, for love, speak treason to thy face?
Open the door, or I will break it open.

Open the door, overconfident, foolhardy king. Shall I, out of love, speak treason to your face? Open the door, or I will break it open.

Enter YORK

BOLINGBROKE.
What is the matter, uncle? Speak;
Recover breath; tell us how near is danger,
That we may arm us to encounter it.

What is the matter, uncle? Speak; get your breath back; tell us how close the danger is, so that we can arm ourselves in preparation.

YORK.
Peruse this writing here, and thou shalt know
The treason that my haste forbids me show.

Read this writing here, and you will know of the treason I cannot show in my hurry.

AUMERLE.
Remember, as thou read'st, thy promise pass'd.
I do repent me; read not my name there;
My heart is not confederate with my hand.

Remember, as you read, the promise you have given. I have repented; don't read my name there; my heart is no longer in league with my hand.

YORK.
It was, villain, ere thy hand did set it down.
I tore it from the traitor's bosom, King;
Fear, and not love, begets his penitence.
Forget to pity him, lest thy pity prove
A serpent that will sting thee to the heart.

It was, villain, when your hand wrote it down. I ripped it from the traitor's heart, King; it's fear, not love, which makes him regretful. Do not pity him, in case your pity becomes a serpent that will sting you to your heart.

BOLINGBROKE.
O heinous, strong, and bold conspiracy!
O loyal father of a treacherous son!
Thou sheer, immaculate, and silver fountain,
From whence this stream through muddy passages
Hath held his current and defil'd himself!

Oh terrible, strong and bold conspiracy! Oh loyal father of a treacherous son! You high, perfect, silver fountain, from which this stream has run through muddy passages and polluted

Thy overflow of good converts to bad;
And thy abundant goodness shall excuse
This deadly blot in thy digressing son.

itself! Your excessive good has converted itself to evil; and your great goodness will excuse this terrible stain in your wayward son.

YORK.
So shall my virtue be his vice's bawd;
And he shall spend mine honour with his shame,
As thriftless sons their scraping fathers' gold.
Mine honour lives when his dishonour dies,
Or my sham'd life in his dishonour lies.
Thou kill'st me in his life; giving him breath,
The traitor lives, the true man's put to death.

So my virtue becomes the pimp for his vice, and he diminishes my honour with his shame, like profligate sons spending their hard-working fathers' gold. My honour will live on when his dishonour is dead, or in his dishonour my life is shamed; you're killing me with his life–letting him breathe, the traitor lives, the true man is put to death.

DUCHESS.
[Within]What ho, my liege, for God's sake, let me in.

Hello, my lord, for God's sake, let me in!

BOLINGBROKE.
What shrill-voic'd suppliant makes this eager cry?

What shrill voiced petitioner is making this great racket?

DUCHESS.
[Within] A woman, and thine aunt, great King; 'tis I.
Speak with me, pity me, open the door.
A beggar begs that never begg'd before.

A woman, and your aunt, great king–it's me. speak with me, pity me, open the door, someone is begging who has never begged before.

BOLINGBROKE.
Our scene is alt'red from a serious thing,
And now chang'd to 'The Beggar and the King.'
My dangerous cousin, let your mother in.
I know she is come to pray for your foul sin.

The scene has changed from a serious matter, and has become "TheBeggar and the King". My dangerous cousin, let your mother in; I know she's come to intercede about your foul sin.

YORK.
If thou do pardon whosoever pray,
More sins for this forgiveness prosper may.
This fest'red joint cut off, the rest rest sound;
This let alone will all the rest confound.

If you pardon anyone who begs you, this forgiveness may engender more sins. If you cut off this infected limb, the rest will remain sound; if you leave it alone it will infect all the rest.

Enter DUCHESS

DUCHESS.
O King, believe not this hard-hearted man!
Love loving not itself, none other can.

*King, don't believe this hardhearted man!
if you don't love your own offspring you
can't love anyone.*

YORK.
Thou frantic woman, what dost thou make here?
Shall thy old dugs once more a traitor rear?

*You insane woman, what are you doing
here? Do you want to nourish yet another
traitor?*

DUCHESS.
Sweet York, be patient. Hear me, gentle liege.

*Sweet York, be calm. Listen to me, gentle
lord.*

[Kneels]

BOLINGBROKE.
Rise up, good aunt.

Get up, good aunt.

DUCHESS.
Not yet, I thee beseech.
For ever will I walk upon my knees,
And never see day that the happy sees
Till thou give joy; until thou bid me joy
By pardoning Rutland, my transgressing boy.

*Not yet, I beg you.
I will always walk on my knees;
and never know happiness again
until you give it to me; until you give
me happiness by pardoning Rutland, my
wayward boy.*

AUMERLE.
Unto my mother's prayers I bend my knee.

I second my mother's prayers by kneeling.

[Kneels]

YORK.
Against them both, my true joints bended be.
[Kneels]
Ill mayst thou thrive, if thou grant any grace!

And I kneel in opposition to them both.

*May things go badly for you, if you show
any forgiveness!*

DUCHESS.
Pleads he in earnest? Look upon his face;
His eyes do drop no tears, his prayers are in jest;
His words come from his mouth, ours from our breast.
He prays but faintly and would be denied;
We pray with heart and soul, and all beside.
His weary joints would gladly rise, I know;

*Is he serious? Look at his face;
there are no tears in his eyes, his please
are a joke; his words come from his
mouth, ours from our hearts. He's only
praying weakly and wants to be rejected;
we are praying with heart and soul and*

113

Our knees still kneel till to the ground they grow.
His prayers are full of false hypocrisy;
Ours of true zeal and deep integrity.
Our prayers do out-pray his; then let them have
That mercy which true prayer ought to have.

BOLINGBROKE.
Good aunt, stand up.

DUCHESS.
Do not say 'stand up';
Say 'pardon' first, and afterwards 'stand up.'
An if I were thy nurse, thy tongue to teach,
'Pardon' should be the first word of thy speech.
I never long'd to hear a word till now;
Say 'pardon,' King; let pity teach thee how.
The word is short, but not so short as sweet;
No word like 'pardon' for kings' mouths so meet.

YORK.
Speak it in French, King, say 'pardonne moy.'

DUCHESS.
Dost thou teach pardon pardon to destroy?
Ah, my sour husband, my hard-hearted lord,
That sets the word itself against the word!
Speak 'pardon' as 'tis current in our land;
The chopping French we do not understand.
Thine eye begins to speak, set thy tongue there;
Or in thy piteous heart plant thou thine ear,
That hearing how our plaints and prayers do pierce,
Pity may move thee 'pardon' to rehearse.

BOLINGBROKE.
Good aunt, stand up.

DUCHESS.
I do not sue to stand;
Pardon is all the suit I have in hand.

BOLINGBROKE.

everything else. I know he would gladly get off his knees; ours shall stay kneeling until they grow into the ground. His prayers are full of false hypocrisy; ours have true passion and deep integrity. Our prayers are out praying his; so grant them the mercy which true prayer ought to gain.

Good aunt, stand up.

Do not say 'stand up'; First say you have pardoned him, then tell me to stand up. If I were your nurse, teaching you to speak, 'pardon' would be the first word you learned. I never longed to hear a word until now; say 'pardon, King; let pity teach you how. The word is short, but not as short as it is sweet; 'pardon' is the most fitting word for the mouth of a king.

Says in French, King, say ' pardonne moy.'

Are you trying to teach forgiveness to destroy forgiveness? Ah, my sour husband, my hardhearted Lord, who puts one word against another! Say 'pardon' the way we say it in our country; the changing French we do not understand. Your eye begins to show pity, let your tongue copy it; or put your pitying heart in your ear, so that on hearing our pleas and prayers pity can make you say 'pardon'.

Good aunt, stand up.

I am not pleading to be allowed to stand; pardon is the only thing I'm interested in.

I pardon him, as God shall pardon me.

DUCHESS.
O happy vantage of a kneeling knee!
Yet am I sick for fear. Speak it again.
Twice saying 'pardon' doth not pardon twain,
But makes one pardon strong.

BOLINGBROKE.
With all my heart
I pardon him.

DUCHESS.
A god on earth thou art.

BOLINGBROKE.
But for our trusty brother-in-law and the Abbot,
With all the rest of that consorted crew,
Destruction straight shall dog them at the heels.
Good uncle, help to order several powers
To Oxford, or where'er these traitors are.
They shall not live within this world, I swear,
But I will have them, if I once know where.
Uncle, farewell; and, cousin, adieu;
Your mother well hath pray'd, and prove you true.

DUCHESS.
Come, my old son; I pray God make thee new.

I pardon him, as God shall pardon me.

Oh the happy advantage gained from kneeling! But I am sick with fear. Say it again. Saying pardon twice does not divide it, it makes it stronger.

*With all my heart
I pardon him.*

You are God on earth.

Apart from my trusty brother-in-law and the Abbot, all the rest who are mixed up in this plot shall find themselves destroyed at once. Good uncle, help to send various forces to Oxford, or wherever these traitors are. They shall not live in this world, I swear, without me catching them, once I know where they are. Uncle, farewell; and, cousin, goodbye; your mother has prayed well, show you deserve it.

Come, my old son; I pray to God to make you new.

Exeunt

SCENE IV.

Windsor Castle

Enter SIR PIERCE OF EXTON and a servant

EXTON.
Didst thou not mark the King, what words he spake?
'Have I no friend will rid me of this living fear?'
Was it not so?

Didn't you notice the King, the words he spoke? "Is there no friend who will rid me of this threat?" Was that it?

SERVANT.
These were his very words.

Those were his very words.

EXTON.
'Have I no friend?' quoth he. He spake it twice
And urg'd it twice together, did he not?

"Have I no friend?" he said. He said it twice and insisted on it twice, didn't he?

SERVANT.
He did.

He did.

EXTON.
And, speaking it, he wishtly look'd on me,
As who should say 'I would thou wert the man
That would divorce this terror from my heart';
Meaning the King at Pomfret. Come, let's go.
I am the King's friend, and will rid his foe.

And, when he said it, he looked at me hopefully, as if he was saying, "I wish you were the man who could remove the cloud hanging over me"; he meant the King at Pomfret. Come, let's go. I am the King's friend, and will get rid of his enemy.

Exeunt

SCENE V.

Pomfret Castle. The dungeon of the Castle

Enter KING RICHARD

KING RICHARD.
I have been studying how I may compare
This prison where I live unto the world
And, for because the world is populous
And here is not a creature but myself,
I cannot do it. Yet I'll hammer it out.
My brain I'll prove the female to my soul,
My soul the father; and these two beget
A generation of still-breeding thoughts,
And these same thoughts people this little world,
In humours like the people of this world,
For no thought is contented. The better sort,
As thoughts of things divine, are intermix'd
With scruples, and do set the word itself
Against the word,
As thus: 'Come, little ones'; and then again,
'It is as hard to come as for a camel
To thread the postern of a small needle's eye.'
Thoughts tending to ambition, they do plot
Unlikely wonders: how these vain weak nails
May tear a passage through the flinty ribs
Of this hard world, my ragged prison walls;
And, for they cannot, die in their own pride.
Thoughts tending to content flatter themselves
That they are not the first of fortune's slaves,
Nor shall not be the last; like silly beggars
Who, sitting in the stocks, refuge their shame,
That many have and others must sit there;
And in this thought they find a kind of ease,
Bearing their own misfortunes on the back
Of such as have before endur'd the like.
Thus play I in one person many people,
And none contented. Sometimes am I king;
Then treasons make me wish myself a beggar,
And so I am. Then crushing penury
Persuades me I was better when a king;

I have been thinking how I might compare this prison where I live to the world; and, because the world is full of people and there is nobody here but myself, I cannot do it. But I will puzzle it out. My brain will be the female to my soul, which will be the father, and these two will create a generation of multiplying thoughts, and the same thoughts will fill up this little world, with temperaments like the people of this world; for no thought is happy. The better sort, like thoughts of heavenly things, are mixed up with scruples, and set one thing against another, such as "Come, little ones"; and then again, "It is as hard to come to me as for a camel to go through the eye of a needle". Ambitious thoughts, they yearn for unlikely things: as if these plain weak nails could tear a hole through the hard stone of this hard world, these rough prison walls; and as they cannot, they die in their prime. Thoughts which lean towards happiness deceive themselves, thinking that they are not the first ones to feel like this, nor shall be the last—like foolish beggars who, sitting in the stocks, consoled themselves that many have and many will also sit there; and this thought gives them a kind of comfort, placing their own misfortunes on the back of those who have suffered before them. So in my one person I play many people, and none of them are happy. Sometimes I am King, then treason makes me wish that I was a

Then am I king'd again; and by and by
Think that I am unking'd by Bolingbroke,
And straight am nothing. But whate'er I be,
Nor I, nor any man that but man is,
With nothing shall be pleas'd till he be eas'd
With being nothing.[The music plays]
Music do I hear?
Ha, ha! keep time. How sour sweet music is
When time is broke and no proportion kept!
So is it in the music of men's lives.
And here have I the daintiness of ear
To check time broke in a disorder'd string;
But, for the concord of my state and time,
Had not an ear to hear my true time broke.
I wasted time, and now doth time waste me;
For now hath time made me his numb'ring clock:
My thoughts are minutes; and with sighs they jar
Their watches on unto mine eyes, the outward watch,
Whereto my finger, like a dial's point,
Is pointing still, in cleansing them from tears.
Now sir, the sound that tells what hour it is
Are clamorous groans which strike upon my heart,
Which is the bell. So sighs, and tears, and groans,
Show minutes, times, and hours; but my time
Runs posting on in Bolingbroke's proud joy,
While I stand fooling here, his Jack of the clock.
This music mads me. Let it sound no more;
For though it have holp madmen to their wits,
In me it seems it will make wise men mad.
Yet blessing on his heart that gives it me!
For 'tis a sign of love; and love to Richard
Is a strange brooch in this all-hating world.

beggar, and so I am. Then crushing poverty makes me think I was better when I was a king; then I am the king again, and in a while I remember that Bolingbroke has taken my kingship, and straightaway I am nothing. But whatever I am, not I, nor any man alive, can be pleased with anything, until he is relieved by being nothing.
Is that music I hear?
Hah, hah! Keep time–how sour sweet music is when it doesn't keep to the beat! That is what happens with the music of men's lives. My situation gives me the sensitivity to hear tunelessness and lack of rhythm; if it wasn't for my current situation, I wouldn't be able to hear the discord: I wasted time, and now time is wasting me; for time is now telling the time by me; my thoughts are minutes, and with sighs they mark their passing in my eyes, the outward sign, to which my finger like the hand of the dial, is still pointing, wiping tears from them. Now Sir, the sound which indicates the hour is the clamorous groans that come from my heart, which is the bell–so sighs, and tears, and groans indicate the minutes, the times, and the hours. But my time is going on without me, Bolingbroke has it, while I stand here fooling, a figure on his clock. This music angers me. Don't let it play any more; for though it has helped madmen recover their wits, with me it seems it will make wise men mad. Yet I bless the heart of the one who gives it to me, for it is a sign of love; and love for Richard is a rare jewel in this all hating world.

Enter a GROOM of the stable

GROOM.
Hail, royal Prince!

Greetings, royal Prince!

KING RICHARD.

Thanks, noble peer!
The cheapest of us is ten groats too dear.
What art thou? and how comest thou hither,
Where no man never comes but that sad dog
That brings me food to make misfortune live?

GROOM.
I was a poor groom of thy stable, King,
When thou wert king; who, travelling towards York,
With much ado at length have gotten leave
To look upon my sometimes royal master's face.
O, how it ern'd my heart, when I beheld,
In London streets, that coronation-day,
When Bolingbroke rode on roan Barbary-
That horse that thou so often hast bestrid,
That horse that I so carefully have dress'd!

KING RICHARD.
Rode he on Barbary? Tell me, gentle friend,
How went he under him?

GROOM.
So proudly as if he disdain'd the ground.

KING RICHARD.
So proud that Bolingbroke was on his back!
That jade hath eat bread from my royal hand;
This hand hath made him proud with clapping him.
Would he not stumble? would he not fall down,
Since pride must have a fall, and break the neck
Of that proud man that did usurp his back?
Forgiveness, horse! Why do I rail on thee,
Since thou, created to be aw'd by man,
Wast born to bear? I was not made a horse;
And yet I bear a burden like an ass,
Spurr'd, gall'd, and tir'd, by jauncing Bolingbroke.

Enter KEEPER with meat

KEEPER.

Thank you, noble peer! The cheapest Prince is ten groats too dear. Who are you? And why have you come here, where no man ever comes but for that sad dog who brings me food to keep misfortune alive?

I was a poor groom in your stable, King, when you were King; I was travelling to York and, with much fuss, got permission to look on the face of my one-time royal master. Oh, how it grieved my heart, when I saw, in the streets of London, that coronation day, when Bolingbrokerode on Barbary, the roan horse– the horse that you rode so often, the horse that I so carefully groomed!

Did he ride on Barbary? Tell me, sweet friend, how did he perform?

As proudly as if he didn't want to touch the ground.

So proud that Bolingbroke was on his back! That nag ate bread from my royal hand; that hand made him proud by stroking him. Couldn't he stumble? Couldn't he fall down, since pride must have a fall, and break the neck of the proud man who stole his position on his back? I forgive you, horse! Why do I criticise you since you, created to be subservient to man were born to carry? I was not born a horse; and yet I carry a burden like an ass, spurred, whipped and exhausted by bouncing Bolingbroke.

Fellow, give place; here is no longer stay.

Fellow, on your way; you can't stay here any longer.

KING RICHARD.
If thou love me, 'tis time thou wert away.

If you love me, it's time you went away.

GROOM.
My tongue dares not, that my heart shall say.

My tongue does not dare to say what my heart feels.

Exit

KEEPER.
My lord, will't please you to fall to?

My lord, will you please tuck in?

KING RICHARD.
Taste of it first as thou art wont to do.

Taste it first as you usually do.

KEEPER.
My lord, I dare not. Sir Pierce of Exton,
Who lately came from the King, commands the
contrary.

My Lord, I don't dare. Sir Pierce of Exton, who arrived recently from the King, orders me not to.

KING RICHARD.
The devil take Henry of Lancaster and thee!
Patience is stale, and I am weary of it.

Made the devil take Henry of Lancaster and you! I am sick of being patient.

[Beats the KEEPER]

KEEPER.
Help, help, help!

Help, help, help!

The murderers, EXTON and servants, rush in, armed

KING RICHARD.
How now! What means death in this rude assault?
Villain, thy own hand yields thy death's instrument.
[Snatching a weapon and killing one]
Go thou and fill another room in hell.
[He kills another, then EXTON strikes him down]
That hand shall burn in never-quenching fire
That staggers thus my person. Exton, thy fierce hand
Hath with the King's blood stain'd the King's own land.
Mount, mount, my soul! thy seat is up on high;
Whilst my gross flesh sinks downward, here to die.
 [Dies]

What's this! Why is death attacking me in this rough manner? Villain, you are carrying the means of your own death. Go and fill another room in hell.

The hand that strikes me down like that shall burn in eternal fire. Exton, your fierce hand has stained the King's own land with the King's blood. Climb, climb, my soul! Your seat is in heaven; while my heavy body falls down, to die here.

EXTON.
As full of valour as of royal blood.
Both have I spill'd. O, would the deed were good!
For now the devil, that told me I did well,
Says that this deed is chronicled in hell.
This dead King to the living King I'll bear.
Take hence the rest, and give them burial here.

Exeunt

As full of bravery as of royal blood. I have spilled both. Oh, I hope this is a good deed! For now the devil, who told me I was doing the right thing, says that this deed has been noted in hell. I'll take this dead king to the living king. Take the others out, and bury them here.

SCENE VI.

Windsor Castle

Flourish. Enter BOLINGBROKE, the DUKE OF YORK, With other LORDS
and attendants

BOLINGBROKE.
Kind uncle York, the latest news we hear
Is that the rebels have consum'd with fire
Our town of Ciceter in Gloucestershire;
But whether they be ta'en or slain we hear not.

*Kind uncle York, the latest news I've heard
is that the rebels have burnt down
our town of Cirencester in
our town of Cirencester in but whether
they have been captured or killed I have*

Enter NORTHUMBERLAND

Welcome, my lord. What is the news?

Welcome, my lord. What's the news?

NORTHUMBERLAND.
First, to thy sacred state wish I all
happiness.
The next news is, I have to London sent
The heads of Salisbury, Spencer, Blunt, and Kent.
The manner of their taking may appear
At large discoursed in this paper here.

*Firstly, to your holy majesty I wish all
happiness.
The next news is, I have sent the heads of
Salisbury, Spencer, Blunt and Kent to
London. The circumstances of their
capture are fully explained in this paper
here.*

BOLINGBROKE.
We thank thee, gentle Percy, for thy pains;
And to thy worth will add right worthy gains.

*I thank you, kind Percy, for your efforts;
you shall be rewarded for them.*

Enter FITZWATER

FITZWATER.
My lord, I have from Oxford sent to London
The heads of Brocas and Sir Bennet Seely;
Two of the dangerous consorted traitors
That sought at Oxford thy dire overthrow.

*My lord, I have sent the heads of Brocas
and Sir Bennet Seely from Oxford to
London; two of the dangerous plotting
traitors who tried to fatally overthrow you
at Oxford.*

BOLINGBROKE.
Thy pains, Fitzwater, shall not be forgot;
Right noble is thy merit, well I wot.

*Your efforts, Fitzwater, will not be
forgotten; I know that you are richly*

deserving.

Enter PERCY, With the BISHOP OF CARLISLE

PERCY.
The grand conspirator, Abbot of Westminster,
With clog of conscience and sour melancholy,
Hath yielded up his body to the grave;
But here is Carlisle living, to abide
Thy kingly doom, and sentence of his pride.

The great conspirator, Abbot of Westminster, consumed by guilt and depression, has given his body up to the grave; but here is Carlisle, still alive, to suffer your kingly sentence, and the punishment for his pride.

BOLINGBROKE.
Carlisle, this is your doom:
Choose out some secret place, some reverend room,
More than thou hast, and with it joy thy life;
So as thou liv'st in peace, die free from strife;
For though mine enemy thou hast ever been,
High sparks of honour in thee have I seen.

Carlisle, this is your punishment: find some secret place, some respectable room, bigger than you have now, and enjoy your life in it. As long as you live in peace, you will die peacefully; for although you have always been my enemy I have seen great signs of honour in you.

Enter EXTON, with attendants, hearing a coffin

EXTON.
Great King, within this coffin I present
Thy buried fear. Herein all breathless lies
The mightiest of thy greatest enemies,
Richard of Bordeaux, by me hither brought.

Great King, I present to you inside this coffin the fear which was hanging over you. Inside here, dead, lies the mightiest of your great enemies, Richard of Bordeaux, brought here by me.

BOLINGBROKE.
Exton, I thank thee not; for thou hast wrought
A deed of slander with thy fatal hand
Upon my head and all this famous land.

Exton, I do not thank you; for you have committed a deed with your killing hand which stains my reputation and this whole land.

EXTON.
From your own mouth, my lord, did I this deed.

My lord, I did this thing on your orders.

BOLINGBROKE.
They love not poison that do poison need,
Nor do I thee. Though I did wish him dead,
I hate the murderer, love him murdered.
The guilt of conscience take thou for thy labour,
But neither my good word nor princely favour;
With Cain go wander thorough shades of night,

Those who need poison do not love poison, and I do not love you. Though I wanted him dead, I hate the murderer and love his victim. You can take guilt as the payment for your efforts, but you do not have my good word nor my princely

123

And never show thy head by day nor light.
Lords, I protest my soul is full of woe
That blood should sprinkle me to make me grow.
Come, mourn with me for what I do lament,
And put on sullen black incontinent.
I'll make a voyage to the Holy Land,
To wash this blood off from my guilty hand.
March sadly after; grace my mournings here
In weeping after this untimely bier.

favour; go and wander through the shades of night with Cain, and never show your face by day or by light. Lords, I tell you that my soul is full of sorrow that I should profit through the spilling of blood. Come and mourn with me for that which I lament, and put on mourning clothes at once. I shall make a voyage to the Holy Land, to wash this blood off my guilty hands. March sadly afterwards; dignify my mourning by weeping as you follow this too early funeral.

Exeunt

The End

Made in the USA
San Bernardino, CA
16 June 2017